Sweet
INDULGENCE

Sweet INDULGENCE

Mandy Wagstaff

with photographs by
Sara Taylor

KYLE CATHIE LIMITED

FOR TIM

First published in Great Britain in 1996
by Kyle Cathie Limited
20 Vauxhall Bridge Road
London SW1V 2SA

ISBN 1 85626 2197

Styling by **Wei Tang**

Home Economy by **Maxine and Jacques Clark**

Edited by **Bud MacLennan**

Designed by **Ann Burnham**

Printed and bound in Spain by
Cayfosa Industria Grafica.

A Cataloguing in Publication record for this title is avaliable from the British Library.

CONTENTS

INTRODUCTION

*S*weet Indulgence is written for anyone with a passion for puddings. If, like me, you crave something sweet at the end of a meal, this is the book for you. I have long had the desire to recapture some of the flavours of my childhood, here by using an abundance of seasonal produce, I have achieved my goal.

These are desserts that stimulate the senses; daring and decadent, they will satisfy even the sweetest tooth. Each one has a strong visual impact and an intense flavour that will linger in the memory long after it has been devoured. From light and fruity, to deep, dark and extravagant there is something here for everyone.

So often the choice of what to cook can be more daunting than the task itself. This book is designed to make decisions effortless, guiding you through the seasons in a natural progression. Each of the four chapters is bursting with the flavours and textures associated with that time of year. There's no need to stick rigidly to my boundaries. If you have a sudden desire for chocolate on a hot summer's day, go for it! But do not be seduced by supermarkets selling strawberries and raspberries, in the depths of winter; they cannot possibly be at their flavourful peak and eating them will only result in disappointment. Nature intended us to have seasons and we should take pleasure in the harvest that each new one brings.

Sweet Indulgence is not about fashions or fads. It is about new recipes, alongside some of the great classics. What unites them is their use of the best seasonal produce to create irresistible, mouthwatering combinations. I believe that over the next few years we will turn away from preserved, processed and packaged foods and resume our appetite for fresh, natural fare. I hope this book will give you the inspiration to experiment with the wealth of produce available to us.

Given the lifestyle of so many of us today, juggling job, family and a hectic social life, making desserts is often reserved for special occasions. What better reason to take the opportunity to make something truly indulgent? Desserts are the crowning glory, the little bit of theatre at the end of your meal. I will never forget at school being told, the word dessert contains two 's' because you always want to eat two of them. How right they were!

Throughout history desserts have been a considered a luxury, devised for pleasure. As far back as medieval times plums, grapes, cherries, apples and pears were grown to adorn the tables of the wealthy. Dried and citrus fruits were imported from Europe along with nuts and spices such as ginger, cinnamon and cloves, all of which are used by us today.

It was not until the 16th century that the importation of sugar or "white gold" as it was often known, replaced honey as a sweetener. It was so prohibitively expensive, its use was limited to the aristocracy and other rich households. Apparently Queen Elizabeth was reputed to have a sweet tooth.

By the middle of the 17th century sugar became more widely available. This was largely due to the English colonists in Barbados turning their land over to the growing of sugar cane. Fine cakes, tarts and biscuits were now being baked in homes around Britain and the first boiled and baked puddings were sampled. Around the same period, ice houses were built in the grounds of large homes and palaces and iced desserts became fashionable. These were often moulded and brought to the table on large platters at banquets and feasts.

During the 18th and 19th centuries desserts gained in popularity amongst all, but the poorest social classes and cooking utensils and cooking methods became more like those we know today. At most middle class dinner parties a grand display of fruit and sweetmeats was placed in the centre of the table and a selection of two or more desserts would be served.

Desserts have been simplified, they are no longer the intricately decorated confections they used to be. Today subtle flavours, textures and colours are the preferred choice. They need not be complicated in order to taste good. This book contains recipes for both the experienced and amateur cook. Time allowing, the more technical puddings can be as exciting to make as they are to eat. Creating something from raw ingredients, and the sense of achievement when it is served, can be very rewarding. I think the most important thing to remember is that cooking should be enjoyable. Do not be over ambitious. Start simply and as you gain in confidence so your repertoire can gain in complexity.

HOW TO GET THE MOST FROM THIS BOOK

When choosing which pudding to cook there are several elements to consider. Firstly it should be in tune with the rest of your meal, providing balance and variety. If the main course is heavy, follow it with a refreshing fruit based dessert, or a syllabub or soufflé perhaps. If you have chosen a dish with pastry, or a rich, creamy sauce avoid repeating the same textures and tastes with the pudding. Maybe a meringue, a sorbet or a jelly would work well. Chocolate is always a popular choice and somehow people manage to eat it, no matter what it has to follow! But bear in mind it can be very rich and filling.

Give some thought to the likes and dislikes of your guests; do they have any special dietary requirements? How much time do you have? Would you prefer a dessert you can make at the last moment? All of these factors are crucial if the meal is going to run smoothly. If you intend to serve a cheese course, my preference would be to offer it before the dessert, I enjoy ending the meal with something sweet, but this is of course, a matter of choice.

Prepare to adapt your menu according to the quality and freshness of the produce available. When you go shopping, keep an open mind. Not only is it important that the fruit looks in good condition, feel it, is it too firm or too soft? Smell it, as this will give a good indication of flavour. Be demanding of your supplier. How wonderful it would be if fruit growers cared more about flavour than heavy cropping. Ask to taste before you make your purchasing decision. Remember if you start with quality ingredients the end result will be so much better. Don't fall into the trap of thinking if it is expensive it must be good. Fruits in season are bound to be cheaper than those imported from the other side of the globe.

The way you present your dessert is crucial to it's success. Remember your guests will devour it with their eyes before they have the chance to eat it. Some desserts look delicious served simply as they are or with just a light dusting of icing sugar; others lend themselves to more elaborate presentation. Whipped cream and piled up fruits can transform a simple cake into a mouthwatering gateau. Chocolate curls add sophistication to a chocolate roulade, mint sprigs or lemon balm give a summery feel to fruit desserts.

These recipes have all been tested and double tested, but everyone's equipment varies slightly, and your idea of a low heat may not be mine. Follow your instincts and adjust cooking times, chilling times and flavourings as you see fit. Unless otherwise stated eggs are size 3, spoonfuls are level and butter is unsalted. Stick to either imperial or metric measurements and not a combination of the two.

RECIPES

SPRING

Spring heralds refreshing citrus fruits. Look out for those from the Mediterranean: flavourful and tangy they are perfect to restore the balance after an over-indulgent winter. Tropical fruits are at their best with mangoes, pineapples, passion fruit, coconuts and lychees. As the growing season gets under way tender pink stems of rhubarb push through. Then comes the profusion of elder flowers to make the most delicious fritters, a wonderful way to end a meal.

LEFT: Rhubarb Alaska

RHUBARB ALASKA

*F*or this recipe you need to select tender young shoots of rhubarb, the pinkest you can find. The forced rhubarb of spring or early summer is perfect. The addition of a few raspberries is to enhance the colour but not intended to distract from the delicate flavour of the rhubarb. A few drops of cochineal can be added instead. If you are serving this dessert for a lunch or dinner party and do not want to be bothered by the last-minute whisking required to make the meringue, I would suggest assembling the whole dessert, meringue and all (this cooked meringue holds up extremely well), then putting it in the freezer for an hour or two which will do no harm. Simply preheat the oven and cook it just before serving.

INGREDIENTS

450 g (1 lb) rhubarb
75 g (3 oz) caster sugar
juice of ½ lemon
50 g (2 oz) raspberries

200 ml (7 fl oz) milk
1 vanilla pod, split
2 egg yolks
50 g (2 oz) caster sugar
200 ml (7 fl oz) double cream

2 eggs
50 g (2 oz) caster sugar
25 g (1 oz) plain flour
25 g (1 oz) ground almonds

110 g (4 oz) caster sugar
2 tablespoons water
2 egg whites
pinch of salt

METHOD

First prepare the rhubarb ice cream. Wash and trim the rhubarb and cut into 2.5 cm (1 in) lengths. Place in a large pan with the sugar and lemon juice, cover and cook over a very low heat for 10–12 minutes. The rhubarb will be very soft and the juices will have run.

With the aid of a wooden spoon press the raspberries through a sieve. Discard the seeds, reserve the purée.

Purée the cooked rhubarb in a food processor or liquidiser. I do this in a few sharp bursts to keep a little of the texture. Stir in the raspberry purée and set aside to cool.

Place the milk and split vanilla pod in a saucepan and bring to the boil. Whisk the egg yolks and sugar until thick and light. Pour a little of the milk onto the egg mixture, stir to combine and then return to the remaining milk in the pan. Cook, stirring over a medium heat until the custard thickens slightly. Do not allow it to boil or it will curdle. Remove the pan from the heat and stand over a basin of iced water to cool. Remove the vanilla pod and stir in the rhubarb purée. Transfer to an ice cream maker and churn until lightly frozen. Whip the cream to soft peaks and add to the ice cream. Churn until evenly mixed and fully frozen. Transfer the ice cream to a 850 ml (1½ pint) pudding basin, cover and freeze until required.

Preheat the oven to 180°C (350°F, Gas 4, 160 Circotherm). Butter and flour a large baking tray. To make the sponge base, place the eggs and sugar in a large bowl and stand over a pan of gently simmering water. Ensure the base of the bowl does not touch the water.

With a large balloon or electric whisk, whisk the mixture until it becomes thick and light; it will triple in volume, become very aerated and will leave a ribbon when the whisk is lifted and a little is allowed to fall back on itself. As a test I lift some of the mixture on the whisk and write my initial across the bowl. If by the end, the beginning is still visible then the mixture is ready. Remove the bowl from the heat and continue whisking until the mixture is cold.

Sieve the flour and ground almonds together and gently fold into the egg batter. Use a large metal spoon or rubber spatula and work with a light, lifting motion. Pour the sponge mixture onto the prepared tray and bake for 10–12 minutes until risen and golden.

Remove from the oven and cool. Cut a disc of cake to fit the widest part of the pudding basin containing the ice cream. The leftover sponge can be frozen or used in a trifle.

Place the sponge disc onto a freezerproof/heatproof serving plate. Dip the pudding basin into hot water for a few seconds and turn out the dome of ice cream on top of the cake. Freeze whilst preparing the meringue. Preheat the oven to maximum.

Place the sugar and water in a heavy based pan and dissolve the sugar over a low heat. Wash any grains of sugar from the sides of the pan using a clean pastry brush dipped in water. Bring the mixture to the boil and insert a sugar thermometer. After 1 minute place the egg whites and salt in a large bowl and whisk, preferably with an electric whisk, to stiff peaks. When the sugar syrup reaches the soft ball stage on the sugar thermometer 116°C (240°F) remove the pan from the heat and pour in a thin steady stream onto the egg whites, whisking continually. Continue whisking until cold, thick and glossy.

With a spoon or palette knife spread the meringue thickly over the ice cream, covering it and the cake completely. Lift up the palette knife to create little peaks on the meringue. Bake for 5 minutes in the oven so the meringue just begins to colour and the ice cream does not have a chance to melt.

This dessert is best served immediately.

Serves 8

RHUBARB CREME BRULEE

*L*ike most people, I adore crème brûlée. This recipe goes one stage further with the addition of one of my favourite fruits, rhubarb. It is like a rather up-market rhubarb and custard. Although a little time is required for chilling, this is an extremely simple pudding to prepare. Once made it can be refrigerated and forgotten until you are ready to eat.

For a more traditional crème brûlée or for those who do not like rhubarb, the fruit can be omitted completely and the rich and creamy custard served alone. This would be perfect for the winter months. Alternatively try using different fruits according to taste and season. In spring scoop the pulp from half a passion fruit into each ramekin before topping with the custard. In summer add a few raspberries or fraises du bois. In autumn add blackberries or blueberries. The variations are endless and can be adapted as you wish.

INGREDIENTS

225 g (8 oz) rhubarb
50 g (2 oz) brown sugar

2 egg yolks
30 g (1 oz) caster sugar
300 ml (11 fl oz) double cream
1 vanilla pod, split

4 tablespoons demerara sugar

METHOD

Wash and trim the rhubarb and cut into 2.5 cm (1 in) lengths. Place in a small pan with the brown sugar. Cover and cook over a low heat for 5 minutes or until the rhubarb is tender. Drain and discard any excess juice. Spoon the fruit into four ramekin dishes.

Whisk the egg yolks and the caster sugar until thick and pale. Pour the cream into a saucepan. Scrape the seeds from the vanilla pod into the cream. Add the split pod and bring to the boil. Pour a little of the boiling cream onto the yolks, stir to blend, then return to the pan. Cook over a medium heat until the mixture thickens enough to coat the back of a spoon. Do not allow it to boil or it will curdle.

Remove the vanilla pod and pour the custard over the rhubarb to fill each ramekin. Place the ramekins on a tray and refrigerate overnight until firm.

Sprinkle 1 tablespoon of demerara sugar evenly over the top of each ramekin and cook under the grill preheated to its maximum setting. Watch carefully; you want the sugar to melt and caramelise but no more.

Chill again for at least 1 hour, preferably longer, then serve.

Serves 4

RHUBARB BAKE WITH A SPICED MUFFIN TOP

This simple nursery pudding would be ideal for a Sunday lunch. The muffin top makes an interesting alternative to a crumble or pie. This type of muffin resembles a cake and originates in America; it should not be confused with the English yeast-based muffins. I always choose the pinkest stems of rhubarb as they give a pretty colour to the finished dish. They are less stringy than the larger green-tinged stems, and taste less acidic.

INGREDIENTS

1 kg (2 lb 2 oz) rhubarb
100 g (3¾ oz) soft brown sugar
zest and juice of ½ orange

250 g (9 oz) plain flour
2 teaspoons baking powder
pinch of salt
1 teaspoon mixed spice
100 g (3¾ oz) butter
100 g (3¾ oz) demerara sugar
1 egg
2–4 tablespoons crème fraîche
** or soured cream**

4 demerara sugar cubes
25 g (1 oz) whole hazelnuts or
** pistachios, coarsely chopped**
** (optional)**

single cream

METHOD

Preheat the oven to 200°C (400°F, Gas 6, 170 Circotherm).

Trim the rhubarb and cut into 5 cm (2 in) lengths. Place in a large ovenproof dish with the soft brown sugar. Grate over the orange zest and squeeze on the juice. Bake uncovered for 15–20 minutes until the rhubarb is beginning to soften and the juices run.

Meanwhile prepare the topping. Sieve the flour with the baking powder, salt and mixed spice. Rub in the butter until the mixture resembles fine breadcrumbs. Stir in the demerara sugar.

Beat the egg, mix with 2 tablespoons of the crème fraîche and, using a fork, stir into the flour. You need a firm mixture that just holds together. Add the remaining crème fraîche if required to reach the desired consistency.

Using a slotted spoon transfer the rhubarb to a smaller ovenproof dish. (It will have shrunk in volume while cooking.) Add half the rhubarb juice and discard the remainder. Spoon the muffin mixture over the fruit leaving the top uneven. Crush the demerara sugar cubes and sprinkle over the top. Add the coarsely chopped nuts, if desired.

Bake for 25–30 minutes until the top is risen and golden. Serve hot with single cream.

Serves 6

RHUBARB FILO PARCELS

These light purse-shaped parcels can be frozen, first on trays until they set hard, then in a bag until required. The succulent rhubarb and melting fromage frais is mouth watering!

INGREDIENTS

650 g (1 lb 7 oz) rhubarb
110 g (4 oz) brown sugar
1 teaspoon chopped
root ginger

50 g (2 oz) butter
6 sheets filo pastry

150 ml (5 fl oz) fromage frais
or Greek yoghurt

METHOD

Preheat the oven to 220°C (425°F, Gas 7, 180 Circotherm). Butter a large baking tray. Trim the rhubarb and cut into 2.5 cm (1 in) lengths. Place in a single layer in a large ovenproof dish. Sprinkle over the sugar and the ginger. Cover with a piece of foil and bake for 20 minutes or until the rhubarb is tender and has released its juices. Remove from the oven, cool and strain. Discard any excess juice.

Melt the butter in a small pan. Lay one sheet of filo pastry on the work surface and brush it with melted butter. Lay a second sheet on top and brush again. Cut into six 12.5 cm (5 in) squares. Place a heaped teaspoonful of the rhubarb in the centre of each square, followed by a teaspoonful of fromage frais or Greek yoghurt. Bring the opposite corners of pastry together to cover the filling and form small purse shapes. Gently twist and pinch the pastry together to seal the parcels. Place on the buttered tray. Repeat the procedure with the remaining pastry and filling.

The parcels can be kept in a cool place for a few hours if required. To cook, bake in the oven at 220°C, (425°F, Gas 7, 180 Circotherm) for 15 minutes until golden brown. Allow three pastries per person.

Serves 6

LIME SYLLABUB

This simple dessert improves with keeping, strengthening all the flavours. It is ideal if you are looking for something quick and easy to prepare a day or two in advance.

INGREDIENTS

zest and juice of 2 limes
75 ml (3 fl oz) white wine
1 tablespoon dark rum
60 g (2½ oz) caster sugar
300 ml (11 fl oz) double cream

METHOD

Place the lime zest and juice in a bowl along with the wine, rum and sugar. Cover and leave to stand for several hours or overnight at room temperature. Pour the cream into a large bowl and add the macerated ingredients. Whisk, preferably with an electric whisk, until the mixture stands in soft peaks. Transfer to six tall glasses and refrigerate until ready to serve.

Serves 6

ICED LIME YOGHURT

This is a good ice cream to make if you do not own an ice cream machine. Although in the recipe I suggest churning it, this is not absolutely necessary. It works very well when placed directly into the freezer because the mixture is already well amalgamated and does not separate, although a gentle beating will give it an even texture. The lime curd can be stored in sterilised jars and refrigerated for a couple of weeks. It makes a delicious treat for tea or can be used as a cake filling.

INGREDIENTS

zest and juice of 4 limes
110 g (4 oz) butter
175 g (6 oz) caster sugar
3 eggs
400 ml (14 fl oz) Greek yoghurt

METHOD

Combine the lime zest and juice in a bowl with the butter and sugar. Place over a pan of gently simmering water. The base of the bowl must not touch the water below. Stir to dissolve the sugar and melt the butter.

Beat the eggs together, then pour through a sieve onto the lime mixture. Stir continually over the simmering water for 8–12 minutes or until thickened. Transfer to a bowl to cool. Refrigerate until required.

Stir the Greek yoghurt into the lime curd and transfer to an ice cream machine. Churn until thick. Place in a freezerproof container and freeze until required.

Serves 8

PINK GRAPEFRUIT GRATIN

*P*ink grapefruit are sweeter than the yellow variety and I think for this reason they are more suited to desserts. The addition of grenadine, more commonly known for its use in the cocktail Tequila Sunrise, gives a wonderful colour and a subtle sweetness to the sauce. Grenadine is made from the sweetened juice of pomegranates. The sauce, or sabayon, should be made at the last moment. Have everything prepared in advance, right down to arranging the fruits on the plates. Then all you have to do is whisk up the sauce, pour it over the grapefruit and grill them when you are ready to serve.

INGREDIENTS

3 pink grapefruit
1 tablespoon caster sugar

4 egg yolks
50 g (2 oz) caster sugar
75 ml (3 fl oz) white wine
25 ml (1 fl oz) grenadine
**150 ml (5 fl oz) whipping
   cream**

icing sugar to dust

METHOD

Pare four wide strips of zest from one of the grapefruit and remove the white pith. Cut the zests into thin julienne. Place in a small pan with the caster sugar and just enough water to cover. Cook over a low heat for 4–5 minutes until the zest is tender and the juices syrupy. Set aside.

With a sharp knife peel the grapefruit, then divide into segments, cutting between the membranes. Drain on kitchen paper.

Bring a large pan containing 3–5 cm (1–2 in) water to the boil. Place the egg yolks and caster sugar in a large bowl and whisk until thick. Stand the bowl over the pan of gently simmering water ensuring the water does not touch the base of the bowl.

Combine the wine and grenadine and pour onto the yolks, whisking continually. Keep whisking until the mixture froths up and leaves a light ribbon when the whisk is lifted and the mixture is allowed to fall back on itself. This may take 15–20 minutes.

Remove the bowl from the heat and whisk until cool. Whip the cream to soft peaks and fold into the sabayon.

Arrange the grapefruit segments in a circular pattern on four large grillproof dessert plates. Spoon a little of the sabayon sauce over the grapefruit. Top with a few of the cooked zests and place under a preheated grill for 2 minutes or until golden. Dust with a little icing sugar and serve at once.

Serves 4

LEMON PUDDING

I have no idea where this dessert originates from but it is one of those popular puddings that is so delicious it is hard to ignore. It is very straightforward to prepare and somehow miraculously, during cooking, the batter separates out to give a rich tangy sauce at the base and a light and airy sponge at the top. When adding the lemon juice and egg yolks to the batter, the mixture usually curdles; do not be alarmed. You have not gone wrong! Add a tablespoon of poppyseeds to the batter to make an interesting alternative.

INGREDIENTS

75 g (3 oz) butter, softened
150 g (5 oz) caster sugar
zest and juice of 4 lemons
4 eggs, separated
50 g (2 oz) plain flour
75 ml (3 fl oz) milk

METHOD

Preheat the oven to 180°C (350°F, Gas 4, 160 Circotherm). Grease a 1 litre (1¾ pint) deep-sided ovenproof dish with a little butter.

Place the butter, sugar and lemon zest in a large bowl. Beat either with a wooden spoon or with an electric whisk until light and creamy.

Gradually beat in the lemon juice and the egg yolks. Sieve the flour and fold into the batter. Stir in the milk.

Whisk the egg whites to soft peaks and lightly fold into the mixture. Spoon or pour into the prepared dish. Stand the dessert in a large roasting tray and gently pour in enough water to come halfway up the sides of the dish. Bake for 30–40 minutes until the top is golden and risen. Serve immediately.

Serves 4–6

ROSACE AU CITRON

When I was teaching we used to make this cake every year for Open Day. In those days we used to make it with oranges but I always wanted to see how it worked with lemons and found it quite a success. Do not expect the rosace to be sweet and sickly; it has more of a bittersweet marmalade flavour.

INGREDIENTS

200 g (7 oz) caster sugar
400 ml (16 fl oz) water
4 lemons, preferably seedless

4 eggs
120 g (4½ oz) caster sugar
120 g (4½ oz) plain flour

250 ml (9 fl oz) milk
3 egg yolks
60 g (2½ oz) caster sugar
40 g (1½ oz) plain flour
a little melted butter

150 ml (5 fl oz) whipping cream

METHOD

Dissolve the sugar in the water over a low heat. Cut the unpeeled lemons into thin slices and add to the syrup. Cover with a disc of greaseproof paper (this helps to keep the slices below the syrup) and a tightly fitting lid. Cook slowly for 10 minutes. Leave to cool in the syrup.

Preheat the oven to 180°C (350°F, Gas 4, 160 Circotherm). Grease and flour a 20 cm (8 in) fixed base cake tin. Whisk the whole eggs and sugar over a pan of hot water until tripled in volume and the mixture forms a ribbon when the whisk is lifted and the mixture is allowed to fall back on itself. Sieve the flour and lightly fold it into the mixture. Pour into the prepared tin and bake for 20–25 minutes. Cool in the tin for 2 minutes before transferring to a wire rack.

Place the milk in a small pan and bring to the boil. Whisk the egg yolks and sugar until thick and pale. Stir in the flour. Pour a little hot milk onto the egg yolk mixture, stir to blend, then return to the pan to cook. When boiling point is reached turn down the heat and cook for 1 more minute. It has a tendency to stick to the pan so stir and whisk it continually. Transfer to a bowl to cool. Dab the top with a little melted butter to prevent a skin from forming.

Whip the cream to soft peaks, then fold into the cooled custard. Drain the prepared lemon slices and dry on kitchen paper. Reserve the syrup. Wash the cake tin and dry it well. Line the base and sides with lemon slices. Chop the remaining slices and fold into the custard.

Spoon some of the lemon custard over the slices in the base of the tin. Slice the cake horizontally in half and lay one half in the tin, cut side up. Dab the cut side with a little of the reserved lemon syrup. Add the remaining lemon custard. Dab a little syrup onto the cut side of the remaining half of the cake and lay it over the custard, cut side downwards. Press gently and cover with clingfilm. Select a plate slightly smaller than the cake and place it on top. Weigh it down with a can of tomatoes or similar. Refrigerate overnight. To serve, invert the tin onto a plate and the cake will slide out. Cut with a sharp knife.

Serves 6

ICED LEMON SOUFFLE

This tangy soufflé makes a refreshing end to a heavy meal. If time permits decorate the top with some candied lemon slices. The difference between an ice cream and an iced soufle is dictated by the amount of air incorporated into the eggs. Here the whole egg yolks are used to give a lighter texture. Always try to buy lemons that are ripe, that is to say they are just going soft, as their juice is better flavoured and there is more of it.

INGREDIENTS

3 whole eggs
2 egg yolks
150 g (5 oz) caster sugar
zest and juice of 2 lemons
300 ml (11 fl oz) double cream

1 lemon
100 g (3¾ oz) granulated sugar

100 ml (3¾ fl oz) double cream

METHOD

To start, you will need a 1 litre (1¾ pint) soufflé dish, a large sheet of grease-proof paper and some string. Ensure the greaseproof paper is long enough to wrap comfortably around the circumference of the soufflé dish and at least 30 cm (12 in) wide. Fold the paper in half lengthways and use to form a collar outside the top of the soufflé dish. It should protrude approximately 7.5 cm (3 in) above the dish. Tie it in place with the string.

Place the whole eggs, egg yolks, caster sugar, lemon zest and juice in a large bowl. Bring a pan containing 5 cm (2 in) water to simmering point. Stand the bowl over the pan ensuring the base does not touch the water below.

With an electric whisk, whisk continually until thick and foamy. The mixture should form a ribbon when the whisk is lifted. This will take up to 20 minutes.

Remove the bowl from the heat and continue whisking until completely cold. Whip the cream to soft peaks and fold into the lemon mixture. Pour into the prepared soufflé dish. Freeze overnight.

To make the candied lemon slices take one lemon and slice it thinly, place in a pan and just cover with water. Cover the pan and cook slowly until the peel begins to soften, add the granulated sugar and cook uncovered for 15 minutes or until the fruits are candied. Leave to cool.

Carefully remove the paper collar before serving the soufflé. Decorate with a little extra cream and the candied lemon slices.

Serves 8

TROPICAL PINEAPPLE GRATIN

When choosing a pineapple, do not judge its ripeness by the colour. Some green pineapples are perfectly ripe. The best way to tell if they are ready for eating is firstly by the smell, which should be sweet and fragrant. Secondly, pull one of the leaves from the top of the plume; if it comes away the fruit is ripe. The addition of rum, which has a natural affinity to pineapple, adds a little Caribbean flavour to this dessert. The dish can be made up and left covered in the refrigerator for several hours and baked at the last moment.

INGREDIENTS

1 medium-sized pineapple
25 g (1 oz) butter
3 tablespoons rum
200 ml (7 fl oz) crème fraîche
50 g (2 oz) dark
  muscovado sugar

METHOD

Preheat the oven to 230°C (450°F, Gas 8, 190 Circotherm). Lightly butter a gratin dish.

Peel the pineapple and cut lengthwise into quarters. Remove the core and cut into 1 cm (½ in) slices. Lay in the buttered dish. Dot with butter and sprinkle with the rum. Spoon over the crème fraîche and finally the sugar.

Bake for 15–20 minutes until the cream is bubbling and the sugar is beginning to caramelise. Serve at once.

Serves 4

BLOOD ORANGE TART

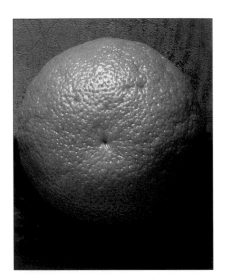

I would not normally recommend refrigerating tarts as the pastry has a tendency to become soggy. But in this case unless you have a very cold larder, I suggest you break the rule. In my opinion this tart tastes really wonderful chilled. If you can't find blood oranges, use any juicy, flavourful oranges that are available. Remember when choosing oranges, or any other citrus fruits for that matter, that size is not an indication of quality. Often large oranges are surrounded by a thick layer of white pith and are dry and tasteless inside. To obtain the maximum amount of juice from citrus fruit keep it at room temperature or warm it slightly before squeezing. This can be done by placing it either in a warm oven for a couple of minutes or in a microwave for a few seconds.

INGREDIENTS

200 g (7 oz) pâte sucrée
  (page 170)

5 eggs
200 g (7 oz) caster sugar
4 blood oranges
125 ml (4½ fl oz) double cream

METHOD

Preheat the oven to 200°C (400°F, Gas 6, 170 Circotherm).

Roll out the pastry and use to line a 25 cm (10 in) loose-bottomed tart tin. Bake blind (page 171).

Lightly beat the eggs then stir in the sugar and the grated zest of two oranges. Add the juice of all four and finally the cream. Stir to blend.

Reduce the oven temperature to 140°C (275°F, Gas 1, 130 Circotherm). Pour the filling into the baked pastry case and cook for 45 minutes or until just set.

Serve chilled.

Serves 8

ICED COCONUT PARFAIT WITH PAPAYA AND LIME

*T*his delicious creamy parfait is rich and full of flavour. The papaya adds freshness and continues the tropical theme. The sharpness of the lime prevents the whole thing tasting too sweet. Coconut powder is available from most large supermarkets these days and is a very quick way of adding lots of coconut flavour to dishes both sweet and savoury. If you have made your parfait a day or so in advance remember to transfer it from the freezer to the fridge for an hour before serving. This will soften it slightly to make slicing easier. Lining the tin with clingfilm is optional but it makes life so easy when it comes to turning out the dessert.

INGREDIENTS

9 egg yolks
150 g (5 oz) caster sugar
9 tablespoons coconut powder
225 ml (8 fl oz) double cream
225 ml (8 fl oz) Greek yoghurt

2 papaya
zest and juice of 2 limes

METHOD

Line a 1.2 litre (2 pint) terrine tin with clingfilm and place it in the freezer.

Mix the egg yolks and sugar in a large bowl and stand over a pan of gently simmering water. Do not allow the bowl to come into contact with the water below. Whisk in the coconut powder. Continue whisking until thick and doubled in volume, the ribbon stage. Do not be surprised if this takes 10–15 minutes.

Remove the bowl from the heat and continue whisking until the mixture is cold. Whip the cream to the same consistency as the yoghurt and lightly fold into the egg mixture along with the yoghurt.

Pour into the prepared tin and freeze for several hours or overnight until firm.

Peel the papaya, cut in half and remove the seeds. Cut the flesh into even slices, grate over the lime zest and squeeze over the juice. Leave to macerate for at least 30 minutes.

Turn out the parfait, remove the clingfilm and serve in slices accompanied by the fruit.

Serves 8

TROPICAL FRUIT SLICE

Puff pastry fruit slices, traditionally filled with soft summer fruits or berries, can be seen in pâtisseries all over France. During the winter and spring tropical fruits make a wonderful alternative. If you have any lime or passion fruit curd, a little spread over the base of the tart before topping with the fruits is a delicious addition. The pastry case can be made several hours or even a day ahead and stored in an airtight bag until required. I prefer to fill and glaze the slice no more than an hour or so before serving.

INGREDIENTS

250 g (9 oz) puff pastry (page 170)
1 egg
pinch of salt

1 mango
1 pawpaw
6 lychees
1 kiwi fruit
1 kiwano or 2 passion fruit

2 tablespoons apricot jam
1 tablespoon water
juice of ½ small lime

200 ml (7 fl oz) single cream

METHOD

Preheat the oven to 230°C (450°F, Gas 8, 190 Circotherm). Butter a large baking tray and sprinkle with a little water. Keep the tray cool.

Roll the puff pastry to an oblong 36 x 23 cm (14 x 9 in). Trim the edges and cut three long strips 36 x 2 cm (14 x 1 in). Beat the egg with the salt and use to brush a 2 cm (1 in) border all round the pastry oblong. Using the back of a fork, make indentations around the border. Lay a long strip lengthwise down each side of the rectangle and press firmly in place. Cut the remaining strip in half to cover the two short sides. You will now end up with a large oblong with a 2 cm (1 in) border all around, rather like a picture frame. Prick inside the border very thoroughly with the fork. Place on a baking tray. Make a decorative edge by pressing two fingers and a thumb all the way round the border. Chill in the fridge for 45 minutes.

Brush with the egg glaze and bake for 20 minutes until puffed up and golden. Transfer to a wire rack to cool.

Peel the mango and pawpaw and cut into even-sized pieces. Peel the lychees and remove the stones. Peel and slice the kiwi. Arrange the fruits in neat rows along the length of the tart, alternating the kiwi and lychee in one row. Halve the kiwano and scoop the seeds randomly over the other fruits. Warm the jam with the water and lime juice. If it contains large pieces of fruit pass it through a sieve. Using a pastry brush glaze the tart with the jam, warming it up and adding a little extra water if it becomes too thick.

Leave to set in a cool place but not in the fridge as this will cause the pastry to become soggy. Serve with single cream.

Serves 6

PASSION FRUIT MILLE FEUILLE

*T*he skin of a passion fruit should be dark purply brown and lightly dimpled. When the skin is very smooth and pale the fruit is often not quite ripe. The flesh inside is wonderfully fragrant and very versatile. I scoop it over all sorts of desserts: meringues, fruit salads, tarts and ice creams to name but a few. The seeds are crunchy and edible although in some recipes such as this one I prefer to sieve them out. The passion fruit curd, as with other fruit curds, can be stored in sterilised jars and refrigerated for a couple of weeks.

INGREDIENTS

4 passion fruit
100 g (3¾ oz) caster sugar
100 g (3¾ oz) butter
3 eggs
juice of ¼ lemon
150 g (5 oz) puff pastry
   (page 170)
1 tablespoon granulated sugar

200 ml (7 fl oz) double cream
2 tablespoons icing sugar

extra icing sugar for dusting

METHOD

Grease a large baking tray and sprinkle with a little cold water. Preheat the oven to 230°C (450°F, Gas 8, 190 Circotherm).

Halve the passion fruit and scoop the flesh into a bowl; add the caster sugar and butter. Stand the bowl over a pan of gently simmering water, not allowing the base of the bowl to touch the water. Stir until the sugar has dissolved. Lightly beat the eggs, then pour through a sieve into the bowl. Cook, stirring continually for 7–10 minutes until the mixture thickens. Add lemon juice to taste. Sieve and transfer to a bowl to cool. Cover and refrigerate until required.

Roll the pastry very thinly to a 30 x 30 cm (12 x 12 in) square. Sprinkle with the granulated sugar and pass the rolling pin lightly over the top. Place on the baking tray and prick well with a fork. You do not want it to rise too much. Chill for 20 minutes, then bake for 15–20 minutes until golden brown. Cool for 1 minute, then trim the edges and cut into three equal strips. Transfer to a wire rack to cool completely.

An hour before serving whip the cream with the icing sugar to soft peaks. Lay one oblong of pastry onto a serving plate or board. Spread with half the curd followed by half the cream. Add a second layer of pastry, then add the remaining passion fruit curd and cream. Top with the third layer of pastry.
Dust liberally with icing sugar.

Heat a long metal skewer either in the gas flame or directly onto the electric hot plate. When red hot press it onto the icing sugar; it will smoke and caramelise immediately. Repeat several times to create a criss-cross pattern on top. Keep the mille feuille in the refrigerator for an hour or so to firm up before serving. If it is left any longer, the pastry will become soggy. Slice with a thin sharp knife using a gentle sawing action. Do not press too hard.

Serves 6

PASSION FRUIT MOULD

I*f you do not have a jelly mould any 1.2 litre (2 pint) mould or cake tin will work here, but choose the most interesting shape you can find. Passion fruit juice, or nectar as it is often called, is available from some delicatessens or larger supermarkets. If you are unable to find any, use a good quality tropical fruit juice instead.*

INGREDIENTS

2 sachets (11 g / 0.4 oz each) gelatine
4 tablespoons water
8 passion fruit
400 ml (14 fl oz) passion fruit juice

50 g (2 oz) granulated sugar
2 tablespoons water
2 egg whites

250 ml (9 fl oz) whipping cream

150 ml (5 fl oz) whipping cream
2 passion fruit
a few mint sprigs (optional)

METHOD

Chill a 1.2 litre (2 pint) jelly mould in the refrigerator. Sprinkle the gelatine over the water in a small pan. Leave to soak.

Halve the passion fruit and scoop out the pulp. Combine with the passion fruit juice. Reserve eight halves of the passion fruit shells.

Warm the gelatine over a very low heat until it dissolves. Blend in the passion fruit and juice mixture, stirring continually. It may be necessary to heat the mixture a little to prevent the gelatine setting as you do this. Pass through a sieve, pressing well with a spoon to extract all the fruit pulp. Discard the seeds and set the liquid aside.

Place the sugar and water in a small pan; cook over a low heat to dissolve the sugar. Use a clean pastry brush dipped in a little water to brush any grains of sugar from the sides of the pan. Increase the heat and insert a sugar thermometer. Cook to 116°C (240°F), the soft ball stage. Whisk the egg whites to stiff peaks then, beating continually, gradually pour in the sugar syrup. Whisk the meringue mixture until cool, thick and glossy.

Whip the cream to soft peaks. Stir the passion fruit mixture over a basin of iced water until setting point is reached. Add a spoonful of meringue to loosen it then fold in the remainder with the cream. Pour into the prepared mould and refrigerate until set.

To unmould, run the point of a small knife around the edge of the mousse. Dip the mould in a basin of hot water for a few seconds and turn onto a serving dish. Gripping both the mould and the plate give one good jerk forward and the mousse will slide out. Pipe a little whipped cream into the passion fruit shells and use to decorate around the base. Cut the two remaining passion fruits in half and scoop the pulp over the mousse. Add a few mint sprigs to make the dessert look attractive.

Serves 8

MANGO AND PASSION FRUIT PAVLOVA

The pavlova originates from Australia where it was created in honour of the prima ballerina Anna Pavlova when she danced the 'Dying Swan' in Swan Lake. Rather like a meringue with a soft marsh-mallow centre and a crisp outside, it was said to resemble a ballerina's tutu. Mango and passion fruit are an excellent spring combination but it is well worth experimenting with other of the many tropical fruits now available in the supermarkets if you prefer.

INGREDIENTS

4 egg whites
pinch of salt
225 g (8 oz) caster sugar
1 dessertspoon cornflour
1 teaspoon white wine vinegar

250 ml (9 fl oz) double cream
2 passion fruit
3–4 mangoes

METHOD

Preheat the oven to 120°C (250°F, Gas ½, 110 Circotherm). Butter a large square of greaseproof paper. Place on a heavy baking tray and dust with a little cornflour.

Place the egg whites and salt in a large bowl. Using an electric whisk beat until they form stiff peaks. Add half the sugar and continue whisking until thick and glossy. This should take 2–3 minutes. Do not be tempted to reduce this time or the finished texture of the pavlova will be spoilt. Add the remaining sugar in a steady stream whilst continually beating. Whisk in the cornflour and white wine vinegar.

Spoon the meringue mixture onto the baking tray and spread to a rough circle approximately 23 cm (9 in) diameter and 5 cm (2 in) deep. Bake for 1 hour; allow to cool in the oven.

Whip the cream to soft peaks. Halve the passion fruit and using a teaspoon scoop out the seeds. Peel the mangoes and cut into long slices.

Place the pavlova on a serving dish. Spread the cream over the meringue. Arrange the mango slices on top and finally spoon over the passion fruit. Chill the pavlova for at least an hour before serving.

Serves 8

MANGO AND PINEAPPLE CAKE

This moist cake with its fruity topping is ideal for pudding or for tea although it is not the type of cake you can pick up with your fingers; plates and forks are the order of the day here. Although one piece of stem ginger may appear to be a bit mean for the topping, do not be tempted to increase it. I have tried and found the flavour takes over, spoiling the subtleties of the mango and pineapple.

INGREDIENTS

I small pineapple, ½ to be used
  for the chopped pineapple
I mango
I piece stem ginger in syrup

150 g (5 oz) butter, softened
175 g (6 oz) soft light
  brown sugar
3 eggs
175 g (6 oz) self-raising flour
3 tablespoons chopped
  pineapple
½ teaspoon allspice
2 tablespoons dark rum

I large tub Greek yoghurt
ginger syrup from jar

METHOD

Preheat the oven to 190°C (375°F, Gas 5, 160 Circotherm). Butter a 23 cm (9 in) springform tin and dust it with a little flour.

Peel the pineapple and remove the core. Cut half the flesh into 1 cm (½ in) wedges. Peel the mango and cut roughly into cubes. Chop the ginger. Mix together.

In a large bowl work the softened butter with the soft light brown sugar until light and creamy. Beat the eggs together, then gradually beat into the butter and sugar. Ensure each batch is fully incorporated before adding the next. If the mixture separates, add a little of the measured flour.

Chop the remaining half pineapple into small cubes.

Sieve the flour with the allspice. Lightly fold into the egg mixture along with the rum and the chopped pineapple.

Spoon into the prepared tin and level the surface. Bake for 30 minutes. Remove from the oven and arrange the prepared fruits over the top of the cake. Sprinkle with the soft brown sugar and bake for a further 20–30 minutes. The cake will be well risen and firm and the fruits soft. An inserted skewer will come out clean.

Remove from the oven and cool in the tin for 2 minutes. Transfer to a wire rack and allow to cool completely. Serve with the yoghurt flavoured with a little of the ginger syrup.

Serves 8

MANGO SORBET WITH COCONUT BISCUITS

T here are many different types of mango, the orangy/red Indian ones being my favourite. The green-skinned variety with a red blush is good too. Whichever type you use ensure the fruit are ripe and juicy. I find the easiest way to prepare them is to take a sharp knife and cut down either side of the large flat central stone, remove the peel from these two halves, then roughly chop the flesh. Peel the skin from the central slice, then cut and scrape the flesh away from the stone.

INGREDIENTS

225 g (8 oz) granulated sugar
250 ml (9 fl oz) water
250 ml (9 fl oz) mango purée
  from 2 small mangoes
zest and juice of 1 lime
1 egg white

2 egg whites
75 g (3 oz) caster sugar
75 g (3 oz) desiccated coconut
25 g (1 oz) plain flour

METHOD

Combine the granulated sugar and water in a small pan and heat gently to dissolve the sugar. Bring to the boil and cook for 2 minutes. Remove from the heat and cool.

Peel the mangoes and cut the flesh away from the stones. Place in a liquidiser with a little of the prepared syrup and blend until smooth. Add the remaining syrup along with the lime zest and juice. Pour into an ice cream maker and churn until semi-frozen. Whisk the egg white to soft peaks, add to the mango mixture and continue churning until frozen. Transfer to a freezerproof container and freeze until required.

Preheat the oven to 180°C (350°F, Gas 4, 160 Circotherm). Line two baking sheets with non-stick baking parchment.

Beat the egg whites with a fork until frothy then stir in the caster sugar, coconut and flour. Place rounded teaspoonfuls spaced well apart onto the prepared trays. Flatten each mound slightly with the back of the spoon. You should have enough mixture for sixteen biscuits.

Bake in the preheated oven for 12–15 minutes until pale golden. Remove from the oven and cool for 1–2 minutes before laying over a rolling pin to cool. (You can lay them flat on a wire rack but I prefer this curved shape.)

Store in an airtight container until ready to serve.

Serves 8

PINEAPPLE MOUSSE

Pineapple contains an enzyme that prevents gelatine from setting, so here chunks of pineapple are folded into a light vanilla mousse which is encased in pineapple slices. Pineapples are available all year but I think they are at their best in spring. Always choose a sweet-smelling fruit with no soft brown patches. Remember to pull away one of the inner leaves from the plume; if it comes away easily the fruit is ripe.

INGREDIENTS

1 medium-sized pineapple
200 g (7 oz) granulated sugar
400 ml (16 fl oz) water
2 tablespoons kirsch

1 sachet (11 g / 0.4 oz) gelatine
2 tablespoons water
2 whole eggs
2 egg yolks
1 teaspoon vanilla extract
75 g (3 oz) caster sugar
250 ml (9 fl oz) whipping
   cream

METHOD

Peel the pineapple and cut into 5 mm (¼ in) slices. Cut each slice in half. Place the granulated sugar and water in a large pan. Cook slowly to dissolve the sugar. Add the pineapple and kirsch and poach gently for 10 minutes until the pineapple is tender. If the core is very tough but the outer flesh feels cooked it may be best to remove the pineapple from the heat and discard the cores. Cool in the syrup, then drain on a wire rack.

In a small pan soak the gelatine in the water. Bring a large pan containing 5 cm (2 in) water to the boil. Combine the whole eggs, egg yolks, vanilla extract and caster sugar in a large bowl and stand over the pan of simmering water. Ensure that the base of the bowl does not touch the water below.

Using either a hand-held electric or large balloon whisk, whisk until the mixture is full of air and leaves a ribbon when the whisk is lifted and the mixture is allowed to fall back on itself. Remove the bowl from the heat and whisk until cool. Melt the gelatine over a very low heat and lightly fold into the mousse mixture.

Whip the cream to soft peaks. Dice four of the pineapple slices and fold into the mousse along with the cream.

Use the remaining pineapple slices to line the base and sides of a 23 cm (9 in) fixed bottom cake tin. Spoon the mousse into the centre. Refrigerate until set.

To serve the mousse, run the point of a small knife around the top edge of the mould. Dip into a basin of hot water for a few seconds, then invert onto a serving plate. Give a good shake and the mousse will slide out.

Serves 6

HOT PHYSALIS WITH PUFF PASTRY TWISTS

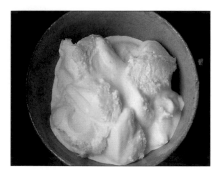

These golden berries are an edible relative of the Chinese lanterns many people grow in their gardens. They are often served as petits fours with the papery husks peeled back and the orange fruits dipped in fondant icing. Here, I serve them warm in a light sugar syrup. I find they are often a little sharp and the addition of sugar enhances their flavour. The pastry twists can be made using puff pastry trimmings if you have some which need using up.

INGREDIENTS

**250 g (9 oz) puff pastry
(page 170)
50 g (2 oz) granulated sugar
50 g (2 oz) finely chopped
hazelnuts
10 g (½ oz) butter**

**250 g (9 oz) physalis
50 g (2 oz) light muscovado
sugar
1 tablespoon water
1 vanilla pod, split**

**100 ml (3¾ fl oz) clotted
cream**

METHOD

Preheat the oven to 230°C (450°F, Gas 8, 190 Circotherm). Grease a large baking tray and sprinkle it with a little cold water.

Roll the pastry to form an oblong 50 x 20 cm (20 x 8 in). Mix the granulated sugar and chopped nuts and sprinkle over one end of the pastry oblong to cover two-thirds of its surface. Press the nut mixture lightly into the pastry with a rolling pin. Fold the uncovered pastry flap over half the nut mixture. Then fold the remaining covered pastry section over the second pastry layer, making a parcel of three layers with the nut mixture in between each layer. Roll out to an oblong 20 x 30 cm (8 x 12 in). Brush with melted butter, then cut into twenty-four strips, each 20 cm (8 in) long, 1.25 cm (½ in) wide.

Take one strip in your hands and, without stretching it, twist each end in opposite directions until the pastry has formed a twist. Place on the baking tray and repeat with the remaining strips. Chill for 45 minutes. Bake for 12 minutes until puffed up and golden. Transfer to a rack to cool.

Reserve six physalis for decoration and remove the husks from the remainder. Place the fruit in a large frying pan with the light muscovado sugar, water and split vanilla pod. Cover and cook over a moderate heat for 3 minutes.

Serve the warm fruits on dessert plates, with two pastry twists per person. Peel back the outer husks of the reserved physalis like wings or petals and use to decorate each plate. Place a spoonful of clotted cream on top of the warm physalis and let it melt as you take the dessert to the table. Hand round the remaining twists separately.

Serves 4

LYCHEES AND RAMBUTANS IN LEMON-SCENTED SYRUP

These delicately scented fruits are a healthy way to end a meal. Closely related with only subtle differences in flavour, these two fruits complement each other perfectly. A light lemon grass syrup adds a fragrant twist. Both fruits come together for a couple of months, with lychee available earlier and rambutan later. With lemon grass, they are all exported from Indo-China and are now to be found commonly on our supermarket shelves. The syrup ie delicately flavoured with lemon grass which has been adapted to grow here now.

INGREDIENTS

450 g (1 lb) lychees
450 g (1 lb) rambutans
2 stalks lemon grass
100 g (3¾ oz) granulated sugar
200 ml (7 fl oz) water

METHOD

Peel the lychees and split down one side to remove the stones. Peel all but six of the rambutans and remove the stones in the same way. Place the fruit in a glass serving bowl.

Cut the lemon grass in half lengthwise and bash it either with the side of a heavy knife or with a rolling pin. This helps to release the juices. Chop it roughly.

Place the sugar and water into a pan and add the lemon grass. Bring slowly to the boil, stirring from time to time to ensure the sugar has dissolved before boiling point is reached. Cook for a further 5 minutes, turn off the heat and leave to cool.

Strain the cooled syrup over the fruits and keep lightly chilled until ready to serve.

With a small knife cut around the circumference of the remaining rambutans, just through the shell. Peel off the top half only and leave the fruits sitting in the remaining half. Place on top of the bowl to serve.

Serves 6

COCONUT RICE PUDDINGS WITH EXOTIC FRUIT

For those of us who were unable to get to warm and sunny climes this winter, here is a little taste of the tropics. As you eat this dessert, close your eyes and let your imagination transport you to a distant place with turquoise seas and coconut palms swaying gently in the breeze.

INGREDIENTS

110 g (4 oz) pudding rice
150 ml (5 fl oz) milk
150 ml (5 fl oz) canned coconut milk

1 sachet gelatine (11 g/0.4 oz)
2 tablespoons water
3 egg yolks
75 g (3 oz) caster sugar
110 ml (4 fl oz) milk
110 ml (4 fl oz) canned coconut milk
50 g (2 oz) creamed coconut
200 ml (7 fl oz) whipping cream

½ mango
½ papaya
½ small pineapple
zest and juice of 1 lime

METHOD

Place the rice in a sieve and rinse well under cold running water. Drain thoroughly and put in a pan with the milk and coconut milk. Bring to the boil, cover with a tightly fitting lid. Turn down the heat and simmer gently for 15–20 minutes until the rice is cooked and the milk has been absorbed. Allow to cool.

Soak the gelatine in the water.

Whisk the egg yolks and sugar in a small bowl until pale and thick. Meanwhile bring the milk, canned coconut milk and creamed coconut to the boil. Pour a little of the hot milk onto the egg mixture and stir to blend, return to the saucepan with the remainder of the milk and cook, stirring over a gentle heat until the custard thickens. Do not allow the mixture to boil or it will curdle.

Add the soaked gelatine to the hot custard and stir to dissolve. Mix in the rice and stand the pan over a bowl of iced water. Stir from time to time to check for setting.

Whip the cream to soft peaks and when the rice has reached setting point gently fold in the cream. Spoon into eight lightly oiled dariole moulds or ramekins and refrigerate for 2 hours or until set.

Peel and dice the fruits. Place in a small bowl with the lime juice and zest and leave to macerate for 1 hour.

Dip each mould into a basin of hot water for a few seconds. Run the tip of a small knife round the top edge of each rice pot and turn onto a dessert plate. Give a sharp jerk and it will slide out. Serve each pudding surrounded with a little of the fruit mixture.

Serves 8

FROZEN NOUGATINE WITH RASPBERRY SAUCE

Nougat has always been a personal favourite and this frozen hazelnut and pistachio nougatine is no exception. If you prefer, freeze it in one large mould and serve it sliced. At this time of year I make quick and easy fruit sauces using frozen fruits left over from the summer harvest; other berries and currants can be used in the same way.

INGREDIENTS

75 g (3 oz) whole hazelnuts
50 g (2 oz) pistachios
75 g (3 oz) caster sugar
3 tablespoons water

225 ml (8 fl oz) milk
1 vanilla pod, split
3 egg yolks
25 g (1 oz) caster sugar

75 g (3 oz) caster sugar
3 tablespoons water
2 egg whites

150 ml (5 fl oz) double cream
zest and juice of ½ lemon

450 g (1 lb) fresh or frozen
   raspberries
juice of ½ lemon
icing sugar

25 g (1 oz) caster sugar
1 tablespoon water

METHOD

Preheat the oven to 190°C (375°F, Gas 5, 160 Circotherm). Place the hazelnuts on a baking tray and cook until pale golden, 4–5 minutes. Leave to cool, then chop them roughly. Blanch the pistachios, drain them and remove the skins, roughly chop them and set aside.

Place the caster sugar and water in a heavy based pan and cook to a golden caramel. Add the hazelnuts, swirling the pan as you do so. Pour onto a lightly greased baking sheet and allow to set. When completely cold break into pieces and crush in a pestle and mortar or with a rolling pin. You should end up with half powder and half larger chunks.

Place the milk and split vanilla pod in a saucepan and bring to the boil. Whisk the egg yolks and caster sugar until thick and light. Stir in a little of the boiling milk, then return to the pan. Cook, stirring until the custard thickens. Do not allow it to boil. Cool and remove the vanilla pod. Pour into an ice cream machine and churn whilst making the meringue mixture.

Place the caster sugar and water in a heavy based pan. Cook over a low heat until the sugar dissolves. Wash down the sides of the pan with a clean brush dipped in cold water. Bring to the boil and insert a sugar thermometer. After 1 minute place the egg whites in a large bowl and whisk to stiff peaks. When the syrup reaches the soft ball stage on the sugar thermometer 116°C (240°F), remove from the heat and pour in a thin, steady stream onto the egg whites, while continually whisking. Continue whisking until the meringue is cold, thick and glossy.

Whip the cream to soft peaks. Fold the meringue into the cream along with the praline, the lemon zest and juice and the pistachios. Add to the custard in the ice cream machine and continue to churn until frozen. Spoon into six individual 150 ml (5 fl oz) moulds and freeze until required.

To make the raspberry sauce press the raspberries through a sieve and discard the seeds; add lemon juice and icing sugar to taste. Chill until required.

Place the remaining caster sugar and water in a heavy based pan and cook to a golden caramel. Using a spoon drizzle the caramel into interesting shapes onto a greased baking tray or a piece of waxed paper. Leave to set.

To serve, dip the nougatine moulds into hot water for a few seconds, then turn onto individual dessert plates, surround with the sauce and decorate with the caramel shapes.

Serves 6

ELDER FLOWER FRITTERS

*E**lder flowers are growing wild all over the place, so even if you do not have your own tree they are easy enough to find, although I would recommend being quite choosy – some of the elder berry trees near us in London are probably so covered in pollution who knows what they might do to you.*

INGREDIENTS

100 g (3½ oz) plain flour
pinch of salt
25 g (1 oz) caster sugar
2 eggs, separated
150 ml (5 fl oz) elder flower
cordial and water mix
(50% water/50% cordial)
vegetable oil for frying
25 g (1 oz) butter, melted
12 sprigs of elder flowers
caster sugar for dusting

METHOD

Sieve the flour and salt into a large bowl, stir in the sugar. Make a well in the centre and add the yolks. Pour the elder flower cordial in a steady stream onto the yolks whilst whisking continually. As you add more liquid gradually draw in the flour; this will give a smooth batter. Leave to stand for 30 minutes at room temperature. Whisk in the melted butter.

Heat the vegetable oil in a deep fat fryer to 195°C (385°F). To check the temperature, fry a cube of bread or a teaspoonful of batter. It should sizzle on contact with the oil and turn golden within 30 seconds. Dip the elder flower sprigs a few at a time into the batter. Shake off any excess then carefully place in the hot oil. Fry until crisp and golden, drain on absorbent kitchen paper and keep warm, uncovered, in a low oven whilst cooking the remainder.

Sprinkle with a little caster sugar and serve at once.

Serves 4–6

SUMMER

Fruit-based desserts are the essence of summer. Here simple preparations make the most of their freshness. Sundaes and sorbets are the perfect coolers for steaming hot days, while baked nectarines or a cherry pie add warmth when there is a nip in the air. As dining becomes al fresco, soft fruits and berries feature strongly. Who can resist the first mouthwatering strawberries as they come into season, or cherries picked fresh from the tree. As the summer progresses fragrant, juicy peaches, apricots and nectarines are plentiful, colourful and scrumptious.

LEFT: Cherries flambé with geranium-scented mascarpone

CHERRIES FLAMBE
WITH GERANIUM-SCENTED MASCARPONE

This is a wonderfully impressive dessert to cook at a summer barbecue. The ideal time would be just as the light is fading so your guests can see the full spectacle of the burning alcohol. Use firm, sweet cherries; the large juicy black ones are best. If you decide to leave the stones in remember the girls can supposedly predict the profession of their future husbands by reciting the rhyme 'Tinker, tailor, soldier, sailor, rich man, poor man, beggar man, thief'. The geranium leaves give a wonderful summery flavour to the mascarpone but, if you have none, use the same method with a few strips of pared lemon zest.

INGREDIENTS

1–2 lemon-scented
  geranium leaves
75 g (3 oz) caster sugar
225 g (8 oz) mascarpone
110 g (4 oz) crème fraîche

1 kg (2 lb 2oz) cherries
2 tablespoons caster sugar
juice of 1 lemon
4 tablespoons kirsch
  or a good slosh!

METHOD

A few days before you make this dessert place the clean, dry geranium leaves in a small container with the sugar. Cover and leave to stand so that the sugar becomes scented with the wonderful lemony flavour.

On the day of serving, remove and discard the geranium leaves and combine the sugar with the mascarpone and crème fraîche. Keep in the fridge until required.

Wash, dry and stone the cherries It is preferable to do this with a cherry stoner so the fruit remains whole. If you do not own one, decide whether you prefer to cut the cherries in half and remove the stones or leave them whole, stones intact. Remember to warn your guests if this is your option.

Place the cherries into a large heavy based frying pan or skillet. Sprinkle over the sugar and lemon juice and cook over a low heat or the barbecue until the sugar dissolves and the cherries are heated through. It is difficult to say exactly how long this will take as it is rather dependent on the heat of the barbecue. At a rough guess I would say 3–5 minutes.

Ensure everything in the pan is hot, have a long match at hand, tip in the kirsch (all at once) and light with the match, being careful to stand well back.

Take the flaming pan to the table and serve from the pan, passing round the scented cream separately.

Serves 8

PUFF CHERRY PIE

If you have the time, home-made puff pastry (page 170) is ideal. Its crisp, buttery texture cannot be compared with the commercial brands. Most people do not have time to make their own and a ready-made packet is an acceptable alternative. There are three main types of cherry: sweet (usually eaten raw), sour (always cooked and often associated with meats), and sweet and sour hybrids (ideal for cooked desserts). For this dessert the cherries should be firm, unblemished and full of flavour. When a recipe calls for ground almonds you will always achieve a better flavour by buying whole almonds and grinding them yourself as required.

INGREDIENTS

450 g (1 lb) cherries
2 tablespoons kirsch

125 g (4½ oz) butter, softened
125 g (4½ oz) caster sugar
1 egg
1 egg yolk
125 g (4½ oz) ground almonds
2 tablespoons self-raising flour,
sieved
few drops almond essence

250 g (9 oz) puff pastry
2 tablespoons cherry
jam/conserve

1 egg

1 large tub crème fraîche

METHOD

Preheat the oven to 230°C (450°F, Gas 8, 190 Circotherm). Halve and pit the cherries and place in a bowl with the kirsch.

Prepare the frangipane in a bowl large enough to take all the ingredients. Cream together the butter and sugar until soft and pale. Beat together the whole egg and egg yolk. Beat into the butter mixture adding a little at a time, ensuring each batch is thoroughly mixed in before adding the next. I like to do this using an electric whisk but it can be done equally well with a wooden spoon or in a food processor. It will be easier to incorporate the eggs if they are brought to room temperature before starting. The mixture should not separate if this is done in stages, but if it does, stir in a few ground almonds or a little flour to bring the mixture back together. When all the egg has been added fold in the ground almonds and sieved flour and almond essence.

On a lightly floured surface roll out the pastry to form a rough circle approximately 38 cm (15 in) diameter. Do not worry too much about getting it perfectly even. Lay the pastry circle on a lightly greased baking tray. Spread the jam evenly over the centre of the pastry leaving a 7.5 cm (3 in) clear rim all around. Spoon the frangipane on top of the jam and smooth with the back of the spoon. Pile the cherries on top of the frangipane leaving the juices behind. Brush the pastry edges with a little beaten egg, then fold in towards the centre allowing the dough to crease and fold as necessary. Cover about half the filling but leave the centre showing. Brush the outside of the pastry with a little more egg.

Bake in the preheated oven for 20 minutes until golden and risen. Turn the heat down to 200°C (400°F, Gas 6, 170 Circotherm) and cook for a further 10–15 minutes. The pastry should be beautifully golden and glazed and the frangipane well risen. Serve warm or cold with crème fraîche.

Serves 10

GOOSEBERRY AND ELDER FLOWER CHARLOTTE

Gooseberries and elder flowers are the perfect combination for a summer day. If you have a glut of goose-berries, make extra purée and freeze it for a late summer or autumn treat. Elder flower cordial is available from many of the larger supermarkets, alternatively you will find it in upmarket delicatessens and some farm shops. You can, of course, make your own by steeping elder flowers in sugar syrup, then straining and storing the cordial in sterilised bottles.

INGREDIENTS

1 sachet gelatine (11 g/0.4 oz)
2 tablespoons water
**450 g (1 lb) gooseberries,
    topped and tailed**
75 g (3 oz) caster sugar
**2 tablespoons elder flower
    cordial**
2 tablespoons water
1 strip lemon zest

125 g (4½ oz) sponge fingers
**1 dessertspoon elder flower
    cordial diluted with
    2 tablespoons water**

275 ml (10 fl oz) double cream
275 ml (10 fl oz) fromage frais

110 g (4 oz) caster sugar
25 ml (1 fl oz) water
2 egg whites

**150 ml (5 fl oz) whipped cream
elder flower heads**

METHOD

Sprinkle the gelatine over the water in a small ramekin.

Place the gooseberries in a large pan with the sugar, elder flower cordial, water and lemon zest. Cover and cook very gently for 5–6 minutes until soft. Don't worry if the fruits break up slightly. Add the soaked gelatine and stir to dissolve. Cool slightly, then press through a nylon sieve. Set aside and do not allow to set.

Brush the unsugared side of the sponge fingers with a little of the diluted elder flower cordial and use to line the sides of a 1.2 litre (2 pint) charlotte tin. You have to balance the fingers in place leaving small gaps between each.

Whip the cream to soft peaks and fold in the fromage frais. Fold into the cooled gooseberry purée.

Place the sugar and water in a heavy based pan. Cook over a low heat until the sugar dissolves. Wash down the sides of the pan with a clean brush dipped in cold water. Bring to the boil and insert a sugar thermometer. After 1 minute place the egg whites in a large bowl and whisk to stiff peaks. When the syrup reaches the soft ball stage on the sugar thermometer 116°C (240°F), remove from the heat and pour in a thin, steady stream onto the egg whites while continually whisking. Continue whisking until the meringue is cold, thick and glossy.

Stir a couple of spoonfuls of the meringue into the gooseberry mixture to loosen it. Then fold in the remainder. Carefully spoon the mousse into the prepared charlotte tin. Refrigerate for several hours or overnight.

To turn out, run the point of a knife round the top edge of the charlotte. Dip the mould briefly into a basin of hot water, invert onto a serving plate and the dessert will slide out. Decorate with whipped cream and elder flower heads.

APRICOT DACQUOISE

The combination of apricots and hazelnuts is always wonderful. Here the slightly sticky meringue and apricot puréee are a mouthmatering duo. Choose small ripe apricots with plenty of pink blush. If possible taste them to be sure they are juicy, not dry and cottonwool-like. Even when fully ripe, I think they benefit from a little poaching as this enhances the flavour. Both the meringue and the cooked apricots can be kept for a few days if properly stored. I think that, once assembled, the Dacquoise is best eaten within 2–3 hours. But a couple of slices remaining in the fridge still taste pretty good the next day.

INGREDIENTS

100 g (3¾ oz) whole hazelnuts

6 egg whites
350 g (12 oz) caster sugar
pinch of cream of tartar

275 g (10 oz) caster sugar
570 ml (1 pint) water

700 g (1 lb 8 oz) apricots
275 ml (10 fl oz) whipping
   cream
1 tablespoon brandy (optional)

icing sugar

METHOD

Preheat the oven to 190°C (375°F, Gas 5, 160 Circotherm). Place the hazelnuts on a baking tray and cook for 10 minutes until golden brown. Cool. In a food processor, finely chop half and grind the remainder. Mix together.

Reduce the oven temperature to 130°C (250°F, Gas ½, 120 Circotherm). Cover two large baking sheets with baking parchment. Grease well and dust with a little icing sugar.

Using an electric beater whisk the egg whites in a large bowl until they form stiff peaks. Add the caster sugar a little at a time until the peaks become thick and glossy. This will take approximately 5 minutes. Mix the hazelnuts with the cream of tartar and, using a rubber spatula or large metal spoon, lightly fold into the meringue mixture. Divide equally between the two baking sheets and spread into 25 cm (10 in) circles. Bake in the preheated oven for 1 hour until the meringues are firm. Switch off the oven and allow to cool inside. When they are cold wrap carefully, leaving them on the baking sheets. Ensure the wrapping is airtight.

Place the caster sugar and water in a large shallow pan and cook slowly until the sugar has dissolved. Turn up the heat and boil for 1 minute, then reduce to a gentle simmer. Halve the apricots and remove the stones, place in the sugar syrup adding a couple of stones for flavour. Poach lightly for 5 minutes until the apricots are just tender. Using a slotted spoon gently lift the apricots from the syrup and allow to cool. Remove the skins.

Whip the cream to soft peaks. Roughly chop two-thirds of the apricots and fold into the cream. Add a little brandy if desired.

Liquidise the remainder of the apricots with enough of the sugar syrup, approximately 150 ml (5 fl oz), to give a smooth purée and chill.

To assemble the Dacquoise, carefully remove one disc of meringue from the baking sheet and place on a serving plate, flat side downwards. Pile the apricot cream onto the centre and, using the back of a spoon, carefully spread towards the edges to cover the meringue completely. Remove the second meringue from its baking sheet and place on top of the cream. Press down very gently. Dust with icing sugar and chill for 1 hour before serving. Pass round the apricot sauce separately.

Serves 10

BARBECUED BANANAS

*A*lthough bananas are not exactly the first fruit that comes to mind when you think of summer, there are plenty of good varieties available at most times of the year. The beauty of this recipe is that you can use firm, slightly unripe fruits and they still give a gloriously sweet end result. Their tight skins encasing all the goodness are perfectly designed for barbecuing. No summer would be complete without at least one helping of this delicious dessert. Simplicity itself!

INGREDIENTS

8 bananas
8 slugs of dark rum
200 ml (7 fl oz) Greek yoghurt
   or 8 scoops of vanilla
   ice cream

METHOD

Have ready a hot barbecue. Separate the bananas leaving their skins intact. Lay them on the rack above the hot coals and leave to cook slowly until the skins turn really black. If you have one of the kettle types of barbecue, cover with the lid to speed up the cooking time. This will take from 5–10 minutes depending on how much heat is remaining in the coals. Turn the bananas over and cook the other sides.

When they are evenly black give each person a banana on a plate. Let each guest peel back the skin and splash in a little rum. Serve with a good spoonful of yoghurt or ice cream.

Serves 8

PEACH MARZIPAN TART

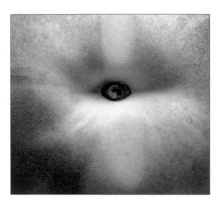

This tart is based on the traditional frangipane recipe used in the Puff Cherry Pie (page 53) but with a twist. Here marzipan is added to the batter to give a softer, richer filling. My friend Teresa inspired this tart. Wanting to make frangipane one day but being short of ground almonds she substituted the marzipan. We ate the finished tart for tea and both agreed it had to be included in this book. For best results choose firm, juicy peaches with a good flavour. There is no need to peel them.

INGREDIENTS

200 g (7 oz) pâte sucrée
  (page 170)

50 g (2 oz) butter
75 g (3 oz) caster sugar
50 g (2 oz) marzipan
2 eggs
50 g (2 oz) ground almonds
50 g (2 oz) self-raising flour,
  sieved

2–3 peaches

crème fraîche

METHOD

Preheat the oven to 180°C (350°F, Gas 4, 160 Circotherm). Roll out the pastry to line a 23 cm (9 in) fluted tart tin. Bake blind (page 171).

Meanwhile, cream together the butter and sugar either using a wooden spoon or with an electric whisk. Finely grate the marzipan and beat into the creamed mixture. Get this mixture as smooth as possible. You may not be able to remove all the lumps, these will dissolve during cooking.

Beat the eggs together and gradually add to the marzipan mixture, beating well between each addition. Finally fold in the ground almonds and the sieved flour.

Cut the peaches into quarters and remove the stones. Cut each quarter into four or five slices, leaving them attached at one end.

Spread the marzipan mixture evenly into the baked tart case. Arrange the peach quarters on top allowing the slices to fan out.

Bake in the preheated oven for 25–30 minutes until risen and golden. Transfer to a wire rack to cool. Serve warm or cold with crème fraîche.

Serves 8

THE RICHMOND GAS STOVE
& METER C.º L.T.º
WARRINGTON & LONDON
PATENT PASTRY TABLET

PEACHES AND RASPBERRIES WITH SABAYON

A *sabayon is somewhere between a mousse and a sauce; an aerated mass of yolks, sugar and alcohol. The alcohol could be a sweet wine or champagne. If you use Marsala it becomes zabaglione. Each wine will give its own distinct flavour. The mixture is not very stable and once cooked should be served immediately. You will find that if it is left for any length of time, the elements start to separate out. Some people add a pinch of arrowroot as a stabiliser, but I have never found this necessary. To serve chilled, continue whisking the sabayon off the heat until the mixture is completely cold, then fold in 150 ml (5 fl oz) whipped double cream. However, I prefer to serve the recipe below hot.*

INGREDIENTS

4 peaches
350 g (12 oz) raspberries
150 ml (5 fl oz) Sauternes

4 egg yolks
110 ml (4 fl oz) Sauternes
50 g (2 oz) caster sugar

METHOD

Peel the peaches, cut in half, remove the stones, then slice. If the peel does not come off easily dip each peach into boiling water for 10 seconds, then transfer to ice cold water and the skins will slide off quite easily.

Place the peach slices in a large bowl with the raspberries and add the Sauternes. Toss well and leave in a cool place for at least 1 hour.

Divide the fruits between six glasses or bowls; then prepare the sabayon.

Place a saucepan containing 2.5 cm (1 in) of water over the heat and bring to the boil. Turn down to a gentle simmer. Combine the egg yolks and sugar in a large bowl that will sit comfortably over the saucepan without touching the water below. Do not put it over the pan at this stage.

Whisk together the yolks and sugar until thick and light. Place over the pan of water and, whilst continually whisking, pour in the Sauternes in a steady stream. Continue whisking until the sabayon is a thickened foamy mass. This will take approximately 15 minutes; and can be done using either a hand-held electric or a balloon whisk. It is important not to stop whisking until the sabayon is ready or the egg yolks will cook and the sabayon will not thicken properly.

As soon as your mixture is ready, spoon or ladle a little over the fruits in each glass and serve immediately.

Serves 6

BAKED NECTARINES STUFFED WITH RICOTTA AND AMARETTI

For this recipe choose nectarines that are firm-fleshed with no bruises. Equally they must be ripe with plenty of red blush on the skins and showing no signs of green. So often fruit sold in supermarkets is unripe; take a wide berth round these fruits as they will never have a full taste. Baking the fruit in this way really emphasises the flavour, the filling adding a subtle hint of marzipan, a wonderful combination. If you prefer, try this recipe using peaches. The white-fleshed ones don't look quite so good but taste divine!

INGREDIENTS

6 nectarines
125 g (4½ oz) ricotta cheese
4 teaspoons honey
pinch of cinnamon
50 g (2 oz) ground almonds
12 Amaretti biscuits
   (6 pairs if you buy the ones
   wrapped in tissue paper)

125 g (4½ oz) soft light
   brown sugar
1 vanilla pod, split
25 ml (1 fl oz) Amaretto
   liqueur (optional)
275 ml (10 fl oz) water

small tub Greek yoghurt
   or crème fraîche

METHOD

Preheat the oven to 180°C (350°F, Gas 4, 160 Circotherm).

Halve the nectarines and remove the stones. Arrange cut side uppermost in a single layer in an ovenproof dish.

Mix the ricotta with the honey, cinnamon and ground almonds. Crush the Amaretti and stir in. Pile this mixture onto the nectarine halves.

Put the sugar, split vanilla pod, Amaretto liqueur, if using, and water in a small pan and stir over a low heat until the sugar has dissolved. Boil for 2 minutes, then pour around the nectarines. Bake for 20–25 minutes basting the fruit from time to time. The fruit should be soft but hold its shape.

Serve warm or cold with a little of the juice and a spoonful of yoghurt or crème fraîche per person.

Serves 6

BLACKCURRANT MOUSSE SURPRISE

If you do not have time to prepare the whole dessert, the mousse alone can be made. To make frosted fruits, whisk a little egg white with a fork until frothy, coat the fruits firstly in the egg white, then in caster sugar. Tap off the excess, then leave on a tray to harden.

INGREDIENTS

1 sachet (11 g/0.4 oz) gelatine
2 tablespoons water
500 g (1 lb 2 oz) blackcurrants
125 g (4½ oz) caster sugar
200 ml (7 fl oz) double cream

50 g (2 oz) caster sugar
2 tablespoons water
1 egg white

1 sachet (11 g/0.4 oz) gelatine
  (minus one teaspoon)
2 tablespoons water
500 g (1 lb 2 oz) mixed
  summer berries
125 g (4½ oz) caster sugar

extra berries
1 egg white
a little caster sugar

METHOD

Combine the gelatine and water in a small bowl and leave on one side. Place the blackcurrants (no need to remove the stalks) into a pan with the sugar, cover and cook slowly for 10 minutes. The sugar will dissolve and the fruit become pulpy. Stir in the soaked gelatine. Sieve the mixture, pressing well with a spoon to extract all the fruit pulp. Cool the purée, but do not allow it to set. Whip the cream to soft peaks and fold into the blackcurrant purée.

Whilst the purée is setting, place the sugar and water in a small pan over a low heat When the sugar has dissolved wash down the sides of the pan with a clean pastry brush dipped in water. Bring the mixture to the boil, insert a sugar thermometer and cook to the soft ball stage 116°C (240°F). Whisk the egg white to stiff peaks. Pour on the sugar syrup in a steady stream whilst whisking continuously. Continue whisking until cold, thick and glossy.

The blackcurrant and cream mixture should be on the point of setting. Stir a spoonful of meringue into the purée, then fold in the remainder.

Pour this mousse into a 1.5 litre (2½ pint) pudding basin. Take a smaller 850 ml (1½ pint) pudding basin and press it down into the mousse. The mixture will be forced up the sides to make room for the bowl.If the second basin is plastic, weigh it down slightly to prevent it from floating. Refrigerate until the mousse is set. Pour very hot water (almost boiling) to fill the smaller bowl, leave for only a few seconds before twisting it slightly and carefully removing it. Your mousse will now have covered the base and sides of the larger container.

Soak the remaining gelatine in the water. Prepare the fruits removing the stalks and slicing the strawberries if using. Place the fruit and sugar in a large pan. Cover with a tightly fitting lid and cook slowly for 10 minutes. Remove from the heat, add the soaked gelatine and stir to dissolve. Allow this mixture to cool completely but do not let it set before spooning into the centre of the mousse. Refrigerate for several hours, preferably overnight. To unmould the mousse, run a small knife around the bottom edge, dip the basin briefly in a bowl of hot water and invert onto your serving plate. Decorate with frosted fruits.

Serves 8

BLACKCURRANT JELLY

Blackcurrant jelly is one of my favourite tastes of summer, the flavour is so intense I find it hard to resist. This is particularly good if eaten with the blackcurrant leaf sorbet (page 66), a combination of sweet and sour. Crème de cassis is the blackcurrant liqueur used to make kir or kir royal, the delicious aperitif. It can be left out, although, personally, I rather like its flavour and find a bottle in the store cupboard always comes in handy. If you make jams and jellies you may well own a jelly bag. This can be used to strain the blackcurrant juices rather than using a sieve and muslin.

INGREDIENTS

**2 sachets gelatine
   (11 g/0.4 oz each)
4 tablespoons water
500 g (1 lb 2 oz) blackcurrants
250 g (9 oz) caster sugar
570 ml (1 pint) water
2 tablespoons crème de cassis**

**few blackcurrant sprigs
   and leaves
single cream or blackcurrant
   leaf sorbet (page 66)**

METHOD

In a small pan sprinkle the gelatine onto 4 tablespoons of cold water and leave to soak.

Place the blackcurrants and sugar into a large pan; don't worry about removing the stalks. Add 570 ml (1 pint) of water and bring slowly to the boil, ensuring all the sugar has dissolved before boiling point is reached. Reduce the heat, cover the pan and allow the fruit to simmer for 4 minutes. Remove the lid and continue to cook uncovered for a further 4 minutes. With a large spoon or potato masher press the fruit against the base and sides of the pan, to help extract the juices.

Place a sieve lined with a piece of damp muslin over a large bowl or wide measuring jug, spoon or ladle in the blackcurrants and their juices and leave to stand for 1½–2 hours without pressing on the fruit. The blackcurrant flavoured juices will drain through into the bowl below. Measure the liquid and add the crème de cassis. You should end up with approximately 720 ml (1¼ pints). Make up to 1.2 litre (2 pints) by adding water.

Heat the gelatine over a very low heat. It is vital that it does not get too hot; a good test is that you should always be able to touch the base of the pan with your fingers, although be very careful not to burn yourself if trying this for the first time. If you are concerned, an alternative is to stand the pan containing the gelatine inside a slightly larger pan of gently simmering water. Either way, when you are sure that all the crystals have dissolved add 150 ml (5 fl oz) of the blackcurrant liquid and stir to combine. If the blackcurrant mixture is cold it may be necessary to warm it up a little so that it blends easily with the gelatine. Pour this mixture back into the remaining blackcurrant juice and stir once more. Pour into a 1.2 litre (2 pint) jelly mould and refrigerate for 2–3 hours or until set.

To turn out the jelly dip the mould briefly into a basin of hot water. Invert onto a serving dish. Holding both the plate and the mould securely, give a good jolt. The jelly will slide onto the plate.

Decorate with blackcurrant sprigs and leaves. Serve with cream or blackcurrant leaf sorbet (page 66).

Serves 8

BLACKCURRANT LEAF SORBET

Atruly refreshing sorbet, and very economical provided you have access to a blackcurrant bush as the leaves are not available to buy. Select young leaves as these give a fresh taste, the old ones tend to be bitter. Do not allow the leaves to infuse for longer than half an hour as the resulting syrup will not gain in strength but will be sour and inedible. This sorbet looks wonderful decorated with sprigs of frosted blackcurrants (see Blackcurrant Mousse Surprise, page 63).

INGREDIENTS

275 g (10 oz) caster sugar
570 ml (1 pint) water
zest and juice of 1 lemon
3 handfuls blackcurrant leaves

frosted blackcurrant sprigs
  and leaves to decorate

METHOD

Combine the sugar and water in a large pan. Add the lemon zest and stir over a gentle heat until the sugar has dissolved. Turn up the heat and allow the syrup to boil for 5 minutes. Remove from the heat and add the blackcurrant leaves and lemon juice. Cover with a lid and leave to infuse for 30 minutes.
Strain through a sieve lined with a square of damp muslin. Pour into the bowl of an ice cream machine and churn until frozen. Transfer to a freezerproof container and freeze until required.

Serve in small scoops in well chilled glasses. Decorate with a few frosted blackcurrants and their leaves.

This is delicious eaten with the blackcurrant jelly described on page 64.

Serves 4-6

CHOUX RING WITH PRALINE CREAM AND SUMMER FRUITS

*T*ake away the summer fruits from this recipe and you would be left with a classic French combination known as Paris Brest. A delicious recipe in its own right and perfect for serving in the autumn and winter months. The addition of fruit gives another dimension. I have tried it with blueberries and strawberries, or a mixture of berries and currants. The addition of a few sliced peaches would be good too. If you prefer, individual choux buns could be made by spooning the mixture well apart on greased baking trays and reducing the cooking time by 5 minutes.

INGREDIENTS

125 ml (4½ oz) water
50 g (2 oz) butter
pinch of salt
pinch of caster sugar
75 g (3 oz) plain flour
2 eggs, beaten
25 g (1 oz) flaked almonds

45 g (1½ oz) whole blanched
  almonds
45 g (1½ oz) caster sugar
2 tablespoons water

3 egg yolks
60 g (2¼ oz) caster sugar
30 g (1¼ oz) plain flour
250 ml (9 fl oz) milk
1 vanilla pod, split
150 ml (5 fl oz) whipping
  cream

450 g (1 lb) mixed summer
  fruits, appropriately prepared
icing sugar

METHOD

Preheat the oven to 200°C (400°F, Gas 6, 170 Circotherm). Grease a large baking sheet and mark a 23 cm (9 in) circle on it.

Pour the water into a small pan and add the butter, salt and caster sugar. Heat slowly to melt the butter. Do not allow it to boil. Sieve the flour onto a piece of greaseproof paper. Bring the liquid to a rolling boil, then quickly add the flour all at once. Stir vigorously to blend and form a ball of dough. Cook over a low heat for 1 minute. Cool for 5 minutes before adding the beaten eggs a little at a time beating well between each addition. Continue beating for 2–3 minutes more. You will end up with a thick, glossy batter.

Place spoonfuls of the batter, just touching one another to form a circle using the 23 cm (9 in) marking as a guide Sprinkle with the flaked almonds and bake for 25–30 minutes until risen, golden brown and firm to the touch Remove from the oven and transfer to a wire rack. With a small knife or skewer prick a few holes in the side of the pastry to allow the steam to escape. Return to the oven for 5 minutes to dry out, then cool on the rack.

While the choux ring is cooking, place the whole blanched almonds on a baking tray and cook in the oven for 7–8 minutes until golden.

Lightly oil a clean baking tray or marble slab. Combine the caster sugar and water in a heavy based pan and cook slowly at first to dissolve the sugar. Brush down the sides of the pan with a clean pastry brush dipped in water. Increase the heat and cook without stirring to a golden caramel. Add the roasted almonds and stir once so they are well coated. Pour onto the prepared tray and leave to cool.

Whisk the egg yolks and caster sugar in a bowl until thick and pale. Lightly stir in the flour. Pour the milk into a pan. Add the split vanilla pod to the milk. Bring to the boil. Pour a little of the hot milk onto the egg mixture. Stir to blend. Return to the remainder of the milk in the pan and cook over a medium heat whisking and stirring continuously, to prevent lumps forming, until the custard thickens and boiling point is reached. This type of custard will not curdle as the flour binds it. Cook for one more minute before removing from the heat. Pour the custard into a large dish. Dab the top with butter to prevent a skin from forming. Set aside to cool. Remove the vanilla pod squeezing the seeds into the custard as you do this.

In the small bowl of a food processor or in a coffee grinder work the almond and caramel mixture until coarsely ground. This is praline. Lightly whisk the cream to soft peaks and fold into the cooled custard along with the praline. It is worth beating the custard well before adding the cream as this makes blending easier.

Split the choux ring horizontally through the centre. This is easiest with a serrated knife. Fill the bottom half of the ring with the praline cream. Pile the prepared fruits on top and finish with the other half of the ring. Dust with icing sugar and refrigerate until ready to serve.

Serves 8

ROSE PETAL SORBET WITH SUMMER FRUITS IN ROSE SYRUP

Y ou may think eating rose petals is a little odd, but try this sorbet once and their distinctive flavour will have you hooked. After all, the use of rose water in cooking is commonplace in Morocco and the Middle East. Choose rose petals with a really sweet scent and a vibrant colour. Deep pink or crimson give excellent results. No need to use those tight buds before they have shown their full glory. The best time to pick them is when they are wide open, just before they start to fade. If you prefer your sorbet to have a lighter texture and a pastel tone rather than deep bubble gum pink, add the optional egg white. If you want to make extra syrup it can be stored for several weeks in sterilised bottles. A little of this syrup diluted with ice cold, sparkling mineral water and poured over ice and rose petals makes a truly refreshing summer drink.

INGREDIENTS

110 g (4 oz) rose petals
570 ml (1 pint) water
200 g (7 oz) granulated sugar
zest and juice of 1 lemon
1 egg white (optional)

225 g (8 oz) mixed summer fruit (strawberries, raspberries, blueberries, redcurrants, blackcurrants etc.)

METHOD

Trim and discard the white part from the rose petals. Place the water and sugar in a pan and bring slowly to the boil ensuring the sugar has dissolved before boiling point is reached. Boil for 2 minutes then remove from the heat and add the rose petals, along with the lemon zest and juice. Stir well and leave to cool. Cover and chill overnight in the refrigerator.

The following day, pour the syrup through a sieve lined with a piece of damp muslin. Reserve 6 dessertspoons of the syrup and set aside. Transfer the remainder to the bowl of an ice cream maker and churn until frozen. If using the egg white, whisk it to soft peaks and add to the sorbet when semi frozen. Continue churning until completely frozen. Spoon into a chilled freezerproof container and freeze until required.

Prepare the fruits according to their type. Divide between six tall glasses, add a dessertspoon of rose syrup to each glass and top with scoops of the sorbet. Serve at once.

Serves 6

BLUEBERRY SOUFFLES

*S*oufflés are not as difficult to make as many people think. If you follow a few basic rules your soufflés will rise every time. *1* Once your ramekins or soufflé dish have been buttered right to the top rim and dusted with sugar do not touch the insides as this will cause your batter to stick in places, giving an uneven rise. *2* Always cook your custard base for 1 minute from boiling – no longer. Add fruit purées or flavourings before folding in the egg whites. *3* Whisk the egg whites to soft NOT stiff peaks and fold them in lightly. *4* Always place your soufflé(s) onto a preheated baking tray which gives an extra boost from underneath. *5* Your guests should always be ready and waiting at the table for their soufflés as the soufflés will not wait for them. This recipe can be made using raspberries or blackberries if you prefer.

INGREDIENTS

110 g (4 oz) blueberries
50 g (2 oz) caster sugar

10 g (½ oz) butter
6 teaspoons caster sugar
125 g (4½ oz) blueberries
6 dessertspoons double cream

2 eggs, separated
40 g (1½ oz) caster sugar
30 g (1¼ oz) plain flour
250 ml (9 fl oz) milk
1 vanilla pod, split

icing sugar for dusting

METHOD

Combine the blueberries and caster sugar in a medium-sized pan. Cover with a tightly fitting lid and cook gently for 8–10 minutes until the sugar has dissolved and the blueberries have burst and released their juices. Watch carefully to prevent them burning. Press through a fine sieve to give a smooth purée.

Preheat the oven to 180°C (350°F, Gas 4, 160 Circotherm). Brush the inside of six ramekins with melted butter. Add a teaspoon of caster sugar to each and swirl it around so it adheres to the base and the sides. Stir the blueberries into the cream and divide the mixture between the ramekins.

Whisk the egg yolks and caster sugar in a bowl until thick and pale. Stir in the flour. Pour the milk into a pan and add the split vanilla pod. Bring to the boil. Pour a little hot milk into the egg mixture. Stir to combine, then return to the remainder of the milk in the pan. Cook over a medium heat whisking and stirring continually to prevent lumps forming, until the custard thickens and boiling point is reached. This type of custard will not curdle as the flour binds it. Cook for 1 more minute before turning off the heat. Remove the vanilla pod.

Fold in the blueberry purée. The batter will keep for an hour or so. It is best to keep it in a warm place as it will make the egg whites easier to incorporate.

Whisk the egg whites to soft peaks. Stir a spoonful into the custard to loosen the batter, then fold in the remainder; don't knock the air out as you do so. Divide the mixture between the prepared dishes. Place on a baking tray that has been heated in the oven for 5 minutes and bake for 12–15 minutes. Remove the soufflés from the oven. Dust with icing sugar and serve at once.

Serves 6

BAKED BLUEBERRY CHEESECAKE

This cheesecake is wonderful if you are looking for a dessert to pre-pare in advance. The flavour matures and the texture becomes richer if stored for a few days in the refrigerator. Ring the changes by using different fruits, blackberries, raspberries and loganberries; a mix-ture of berries and currants works well too.

INGREDIENTS

110 g (4 oz) digestive biscuits
50 g (2 oz) butter

250 g (9 oz) curd cheese
250 g (9 oz) cream cheese
zest of 1 lemon
juice of ½ lemon
3 small eggs, beaten
125 g (4½ oz) caster sugar
seeds from 1 vanilla pod
350 g (12 oz) blueberries
1 dessertspoon plain flour

icing sugar

METHOD

Lightly butter a 22 cm (8½ in) springform tin; dust with flour. Preheat the oven to 180°C (350°F, Gas 4, 160 Circotherm).

Break the biscuits into a food processor and work to the texture of coarse sand. Alternatively place them in a bowl and crush with the end of a rolling pin or pestle. Melt the butter and stir into the biscuit crumbs until they are evenly coated. Spread the mixture to cover the base of the prepared tin, pressing down well. Chill whilst making the cheesecake batter.

Sieve the cheeses together into a large bowl. Add the lemon zest and juice, beaten eggs, caster sugar and the seeds from the vanilla pod. Beat well to form a smooth batter. Wash the blueberries and dry on kitchen paper, toss with the flour and fold into the cheeses. Pour this mixture into the biscuit-lined tin and bake for 35–40 minutes, until firm. Turn the oven off and, leaving the door ajar, allow the cheesecake to cool inside. Chill, preferably overnight.

To serve the cheesecake, loosen the sides with a palette knife and carefully unclip the tin. Slide the palette knife between the base and the biscuit layer and transfer onto your serving plate. Dust with icing sugar and cut into wedges.

Serves 8–10

SUMMER FRUIT SLICE

T his dessert always reminds me of cream teas as the base mixture tastes rather like a scone dough. It is quick and simple to prepare and can be topped with a variety of fruits and berries, or just one type if you prefer. For real indulgence serve with clotted cream rather than *crème fraîche*.

INGREDIENTS

100 g (3¾ oz) self-raising flour
½ teaspoon baking powder
40 g (1½ oz) butter
30 g (1¼ oz) soft light
  brown sugar
1 egg
1 tablespoon milk
15 g (½ oz) flaked almonds
1 dessertspoon soft light
  brown sugar

3 tablespoons redcurrant jelly
450 g (1 lb) mixed fruits
  eg strawberries, blueberries,
  redcurrants, blackberries,
  raspberries

small tub crème fraîche

METHOD

Preheat the oven to 190°C (375°F, Gas 5, 160 Circotherm). Butter and flour a 23 cm (9 in) shallow cake tin.

Sieve the flour and baking powder into a bowl. Rub in the butter and add the sugar. Combine the egg and milk in a jug and blend with a fork. Working quickly stir the liquid into the flour mixture and mix well.

Spread the mixture into the prepared tin and sprinkle with the almonds and dessertspoon of sugar. Bake for 15 minutes until risen and golden. Remove from the oven and transfer to a wire rack to cool.

Heat the redcurrant jelly in a small pan until warm and liquid. Glaze the top of the cake with a little jelly, leaving a clear 2.5 cm (1 in) rim around the edge. The jelly helps the fruit to stick. Arrange the fruit on top and glaze again, reheating the jelly if necessary.

Serve in slices with the crème fraîche.

Serves 6

RASPBERRY BRULEE TART

This is a bit of a cheat's Crème Brûlée; normally it would be made with egg yolks and all double cream. The omission of the eggs and the use of Greek yoghurt gives an altogether lighter and fresher tart ideal for summer eating. I like to serve it in the tart case although it can be made very quickly by simply placing the filling in a gratin dish instead. When grilling the tart you may find it necessary to protect the edges of the pastry with a collar of tin foil. This will prevent them getting excessively brown.

INGREDIENTS

200 g (7 oz) plain flour
pinch of salt
100 g (3¾ oz) butter
1 teaspoon vanilla essence
45 g (1½ oz) icing sugar
2 egg yolks
1 dessertspoon water

1 egg, beaten

25 g (1 oz) ground almonds
300 g (11 oz) raspberries
zest of 1 orange
1 tablespoon caster sugar
150 ml (5 fl oz) double cream
150 ml (5 fl oz) Greek yoghurt
50 g (2 oz) demerara sugar

METHOD

To make the pastry, sift the flour and salt into a food processor. Add the diced butter and vanilla essence and process until the mixture resembles fine breadcrumbs. Sieve in the icing sugar and add the egg yolks along with the cold water. Process to a smooth dough. Wrap in clingfilm and chill for at least 1 hour.

Preheat the oven to 180°C (350°F, Gas 4, 160 Circotherm).

On a lightly floured surface roll the dough to a circle and use to line a 23 cm (9 in) round, loose-bottomed tart tin. Prick the base and bake blind (page 171) for 10 minutes. Remove the baking beans and cook for a further 10 minutes. Brush the base and sides of the pastry case with beaten egg and return to the oven for 1 minute. Repeat once more. Cool.

Sprinkle the almonds over the base of the pastry case. Place the raspberries on top. Cover evenly with the orange zest and the caster sugar.

Lightly whip the cream and mix with the Greek yoghurt. Spread this mixture over the raspberries to cover them evenly. Chill for 30 minutes.

Preheat the grill to its maximum setting. Place the tart on a baking tray. Sprinkle over the demerara sugar to cover the cream completely. Place under the grill for 4–6 minutes until the top is golden brown and just beginning to caramelise. Remove from the grill and chill for 1 hour before serving.

Serves 6

FLOATING ISLANDS ON BERRY COMPOTE

Floating Islands are traditionally served on a pool of vanilla custard. Here I have chosen to combine them with a summer berry compôte. If the prospect of making angel hair or spun sugar fills you with horror a simple alternative is to spoon a little caramel onto waxed paper to form weird and wonderful shapes. These will quickly harden and can be stuck into the meringue to give a pretty decoration.

INGREDIENTS

1 kg (2 lb 2 oz) mixed summer fruit (strawberries, rasp-berries, blackcurrants, red-currants, blueberries, tay-berries, loganberries, black-berries, cherries etc.)
125 g (4½ oz) caster sugar
3 tablespoons water
2 teaspoons arrowroot blended with 2 tablespoons water

6 egg whites
pinch of salt
275 g (10 oz) caster sugar
570 ml (1 pint) milk
570 ml (1 pint) water

90 g (3½ oz) granulated sugar
2 tablespoons water

METHOD

Prepare all the fruits hulling, de-stringing and stoning them as required. Put them in a large pan, add the caster sugar and water. Cook over a moderate heat for 2–3 minutes until the sugar dissolves and the currants just begin to burst. Add the blended arrowroot to the fruit mixture in the pan, stir and cook for 1 minute until thickened. Transfer to a bowl to cool.

In a large bowl using an electric whisk, beat the egg whites with the salt until they form stiff peaks. Gradually add half the caster sugar and continue beating until very firm, 3–5 minutes. Fold in the remaining sugar.

Heat the milk and water in a large shallow pan until it just begins to simmer, it must not boil violently. Using two tablespoons, take heaped spoonfuls of the meringue mixture and shape into quenelles or egg shapes. Drop them into the hot milk and poach for 3 minutes, then turn them over and cook on the other side for a further 3 minutes. Do not put too many in the pan at once as they puff up and become difficult to turn over.

With a slotted spoon transfer the meringues to a double layer of kitchen paper or a clean tea towel to drain and cool. You will have to cook the meringues in two or three stages. Depending on how generous your spoonfuls are, you should have enough mixture to make sixteen to twenty meringues. Allow two per person.

When all the meringues are cooked and cooled, pile them on top of the berries and chill until ready to serve.

Just before serving, place the granulated sugar and water in a small heavy based pan. Cook slowly until the sugar has dissolved. Use a clean pastry brush dipped in a little water to wash down any grains of sugar that may have stuck to the sides of the pan. Increase the heat and, without stirring, allow the sugar syrup to cook to a golden caramel. Do not leave the pan at any stage during this time unless you really know what you are doing as once the caramel starts to brown it will burn very quickly. As soon as the caramel is the desired colour, arrest the cooking by dipping the base of the pan in a basin of cold water for a few seconds. Don't be alarmed: it will sizzle and hiss for a moment.

Take a fork with well defined prongs. Dip it into the caramel, then quickly draw it out. Long fine threads will start to form. Wind the fork around the dessert letting the angel hair fall onto the meringues. Keep dipping the fork into the caramel and pulling out the threads until you have a good coating. It may be necessary to warm the caramel over a low heat from time to time.

If you want your angel hair to have a cage-like shape, lightly grease the outside of an upturned pudding basin, wind the fork around the basin allowing several layers of sugar to build up. Leave to harden for a few seconds, then carefully lift the sugar cage off the bowl and place it over the dessert.

Angel hair will normally last for 45 minutes to 1 hour. However on a wet or damp day this time is often reduced to 20–30 minutes. As the sugar absorbs moisture from the air it becomes sticky and liquid again.

Serves 8–10

MINT ICE CREAM

Mint is one of the easiest herbs to grow. A really good handful of fresh and fragrant leaves to give a powerful flavour. Try different types; peppermint, spearmint, pineapple mint and gingermint all have their own unique tastes. You can put the ice cream into lolly moulds for a summertime treat for children.

INGREDIENTS

250 ml (9 fl oz) milk
3 egg yolks
60 g (2½ oz) caster sugar
a large handful of mint leaves
125 ml (4½ fl oz) double
  cream

METHOD

Place the milk in a small pan and bring to the boil. Meanwhile whisk the egg yolks and sugar in a bowl until thick and pale. Pour on a little of the hot milk, stir to blend then return to the pan with the remainder of the milk. Cook, stirring, over a medium heat until the custard thickens to lightly coat the back of a spoon. Do not allow it to boil or it will curdle. Leave to cool slightly.

Place the mint in a blender or food processor, add a little custard and process until smooth. Pass through a sieve to remove any large pieces of mint that still remain. Mix with the remaining custard. Lightly whip the cream and fold into the mint custard. Pour into an ice cream machine and churn until frozen.

Serves 6 or makes 6 lollies

STRAWBERRY SUNDAE

For this recipe I like to choose large ripe juicy berries; Cambridge Favourite is a commonly grown variety which would work well here. Adding icing sugar to the purée really enhances the strawberry flavour; you should not need more than 50–100 g (2–4 oz) depending on the initial sweetness of the fruit. Add it slowly and keep testing until it gives a deep, well-rounded taste. Everythingcan be made in advance. The meringues keep well in an airtight tin. The ice cream can be stored for 1–2 weeks in the freezer. If it becomes a little hard simply transfer to the fridge to soften for an hour or so before serving. Even the purée can be made in advance and frozen or kept covered in the refrigerator for several days, leaving just the assembling for the day of serving.

INGREDIENTS

2 egg whites
pinch of salt
110 g (4 oz) caster sugar

700 g (1 lb 8 oz) strawberries
juice of ½ lemon
icing sugar to taste
225 ml (8 fl oz) whipping
  cream

175 ml (6 fl oz) whipping
  cream
8 large strawberries
8 sprigs of mint or borage

METHOD

Preheat the oven to 130°C (250°F, Gas ½, 120 Circotherm). Line two baking trays with baking parchment.

Firstly prepare the meringues. Place the egg whites in a large bowl along with the salt. (Salt helps to break down the egg white.) Using an electric beater, whisk into stiff peaks. Add half the caster sugar and continue whisking until thick and glossy, 2–3 minutes. Add the remaining sugar in a steady stream whilst continually beating. Fill the meringue into a piping bag fitted with a medium-size fluted nozzle. Pipe 5 cm (2 in) meringues evenly spaced onto the baking parchment. You will have approximately twenty-four meringues. Bake in the preheated oven for 45 minutes. Turn off the oven and allow the meringues to cool inside. Store in an airtight container until required.

Wipe, hull and halve the strawberries and place in a blender or food processor along with the lemon juice. Process until roughly chopped then add the icing sugar; add enough to bring out the full flavour of the strawberries. Process for a few seconds more. You will have about 850 ml (1½ pints) of purée.

Reserve 275 ml (½ pint) of the purée and refrigerate until required. Place the remainder in the bowl of an ice cream machine with the cream. Churn until frozen. Transfer to a freezeproof container and freeze until required.

Chill eight tall glasses on a tray in the refrigerator for 15 minutes. Lightly whip the remaining cream to soft peaks. Place a small scoop of ice cream in the base of each glass, add a crushed meringue, top with a spoonful of cream and a drizzle of the reserved strawberry purée. Repeat with two more layers of each. Place a strawberry and a sprig of mint or borage on top of each sundae and serve immediately with long spoons.

Serves 8

STRAWBERRY AND CREAM JELLY

*T*his is the true taste of summer. Although it takes a little time to prepare it is a sparkling jewel on a summer day. Choose a variety of strawberry with a really full flavour. If you do not grow your own fruit, going to a pick-your-own farm is the best option. Select small but fully ripe berries with a fresh green calyx. Remember, unless absolutely necessary, do not wash strawberries as they soak up the water, spoiling the delicate texture and flavour. Just wipe and hull them and they are ready to use.

INGREDIENTS

600 g (1 lb 5 oz) strawberries
juice of ½ lemon
25 g (1 oz) icing sugar

1 sachet (11 g/0.4 oz) gelatine
2 tablespoons water

475 ml (17 fl oz) rosé wine
90 g (3½ oz) caster sugar

1 sachet (11 g/0.4 oz) gelatine
2 tablespoons water
1 whole egg
1 egg yolk
50 g (2 oz) caster sugar
75 ml (3 fl oz) double cream

METHOD

Wipe and hull the strawberries and cut in half. Reserve 350 g (12 oz) of the best looking halves and purée the remainder with a few drops of lemon juice and the icing sugar in a food processor or blender. Pass through a sieve to remove the seeds. Put aside.

Soak the first sachet of gelatine in the water in a ramekin or small dish. Heat the wine and bring to the boil, remove from the heat and stir in the caster sugar and gelatine. When both are completely dissolved add a few drops of lemon juice. Pour a thin layer of the jelly just to cover the base of a 1.2 litre (2 pint) terrine tin and refrigerate until set.

Leave the remaining jelly at room temperature. Do not allow it to set. Remove the terrine from the fridge and add half the strawberries in a single layer. Remember the bottom will be the top when the dessert is turned out, so arrange them neatly. Pour on enough of the unset jelly to just cover the strawberries and chill again until set.

Meanwhile make the mousse. Soak the second sachet of gelatine in the water in a small pan. Put the whole egg, the egg yolk and the sugar in a large bowl. Stand the bowl over a pan of gently simmering water, ensuring that the base of the bowl does not actually touch the water. Whisk vigorously either with a balloon whisk or hand-held electric whisk until thick and light. A ribbon will form when a little of the mixture is allowed to fall back on itself. Heat the gelatine over a very low heat to dissolve it. Stir into the strawberry purée, then fold into the mousse mixture. Whip the cream to soft peaks then fold into the mousse. Pour the mousse onto the now firm strawberry jelly and set in the refrigerator. The terrine tin will now be two-thirds full.

When the mousse is firm arrange the remaining strawberry halves on top. Pour on the remaining unset jelly which will be just enough to cover the fruit.

Chill again until ready to serve. If the jelly sets before you have poured on the final layer heat it very gently until it becomes liquid again. Ensure it is not hot when you pour it onto the mousse or you will melt it.

To unmould the jelly, run the point of a small knife around the top edge to loosen it. Dip the terrine tin into a basin of hot water for a few seconds. Invert it onto a serving plate and give one firm jolt to release it from the tin. Do not hold it in the hot water for too long or the jelly will melt.

Serves 6

MINTED STRAWBERRIES WITH CLOTTED CREAM AND SPICE SNAPS

The recipe for spice snaps is based on one for brandy snaps. For this particular recipe I like to keep the biscuits flat, layering them with the fruit and cream. The addition of balsamic vinegar and black pepper to strawberries enhances the flavour. I often sprinkle a little directly onto a bowl of strawberries and cream. The mint adds a refreshing summery touch.

INGREDIENTS

50 g (2 oz) plain flour
½ teaspoon mixed spice
50 g (2 oz) butter
50 g (2 oz) caster sugar
1½ tablespoons golden syrup

1 kg (2 lb 2 oz) strawberries
50 g (2 oz) caster sugar
110 ml (4 fl oz) water
juice of ½ lemon
few sprigs fresh mint
1 teaspoon balsamic vinegar
freshly ground black pepper

6 dessertspoons clotted cream

mint sprigs

METHOD

Preheat the oven to 200°C (400°F, Gas 6, 170 Circotherm). Line two large baking sheets with non-stick baking parchment.

Sieve together the flour and mixed spice. In a small pan over a low heat, cook the butter, sugar and syrup until the butter has melted and the sugar dissolved. Remove from the heat and cool slightly before stirring in the flour.

Place level teaspoons of the mixture spaced at least 10 cm (4 in) apart onto the prepared baking trays. There should be enough batter to make eighteen biscuits. Bake for 7–8 minutes until a rich golden colour with a bubbly texture. Remove the trays from the oven and leave for 1 minute before transferring the biscuits to a wire rack to cool. As soon as they are cold place them in an air-tight container until required.

Wipe and hull the strawberries and cut any large ones in halves or quarters. Place the sugar and cold water in a pan. Cook slowly to dissolve the sugar. Turn up the heat and boil for 2 minutes. Cool slightly. Place one third of the strawberries into a liquidiser or food processor, pour on the syrup and add the lemon juice, mint, balsamic vinegar and a few grinds of black pepper. Process to a smooth purée.

Assemble the dessert just before serving. Place a biscuit on each of six dessert plates. Divide the prepared strawberries between the six biscuits allowing them to tumble over onto the plates. Add a spoonful of strawberry purée, top with another biscuit, then with a layer of clotted cream. Add a further spoonful of strawberry purée to each and finally another biscuit. Drizzle any remaining purée onto the plate. Decorate with mint sprigs and serve.

Serves 6

STRAWBERRY DREAM GATEAU

This dreamy gâteau is perfect for a summer lunch party or afternoon tea. Fraise des bois are wild alpine strawberries and have a particularly delicious flavour. They are extremely easy to grow in the garden but if you do not have such a luxury and find they are too expensive to buy from the shops, raspberries make a good alternative. When moistening the cake with the syrup (I do this with a clean pastry brush) be careful not to make the sponge soggy by being over-generous. A little dab here and there will suffice.

INGREDIENTS

5 eggs
150 g (5 oz) caster sugar
75 g (3 oz) plain flour
75 g (3 oz) ground hazelnuts

50 g (2 oz) caster sugar
110 ml (4 fl oz) water
**1 tablespoon strawberry
  eau-de-vie (optional)**

275 ml (10 fl oz) double cream
50 g (2 oz) icing sugar, sieved

450 g (1 lb) strawberries, sliced
250 g (9 oz) fraise des bois
4 tablespoons strawberry jam

whipping cream
180 g (6 oz) strawberries
125 g (4½ oz) fraise des bois
icing sugar

METHOD

Preheat the oven to 180°C (350°F, Gas 4, 160 Circotherm). Butter a 23 cm (9 in) cake tin, line the base with a disc of buttered greaseproof paper and dust the tin lightly with flour.

Heat a large pan containing 5 cm (2 in) water until it is gently simmering. Place the eggs and caster sugar in a large bowl. Whisk together, then stand over the pan of water, ensuring that the bowl does not touch the water below. With a hand-held electric or balloon whisk, whisk until the mixture is thick and pale and tripled in volume. This is the ribbon stage. To check you have reached it, lift the whisk and allow the mixture to fall back on itself; it should form thick ribbons. Remove the bowl from the pan and continue whisking until the mixture is completely cold.

Sieve together the flour and ground hazelnuts and carefully fold into the mixture using a figure of eight motion. Try not to knock the air out of the batter as you do this. Pour the mixture into the prepared tin and bake for 20–25 minutes until well risen and golden. If the cake is just beginning to come away from the sides of the tin and is springy to the touch then it is cooked.

Remove from the oven and leave the cake in the tin for 2 minutes before transferring to a wire rack to cool. Be sure to cool it with the top side uppermost.

Whilst the cake is cooling, dissolve the caster sugar in the water over a gentle heat, bring to the boil and cook for 2 minutes. Add the eau-de-vie, if desired, then cool the syrup.

Place the double cream and sieved icing sugar in a bowl and whisk to soft peaks.

Wipe, hull and slice the strawberries and pick over the fraise des bois. Mix together.

When the cake is cool, use a serrated knife to cut it horizontally into three equal layers. Before separating the layers, I make an identifying mark on each one so it is easy to line them up when rebuilding the cake. Remove the top two layers of cake and place the bottom layer onto a serving plate. Dab the cut sponge with a little syrup to moisten it. Carefully spread half the strawberry jam evenly over the cake. Top with half the sweetened cream spreading it right to the edges. Finally add half the sliced strawberries and fraise des bois. Repeat the process with the middle layer of cake, adding syrup, jam, cream and fruit. Dab the underside (cut face) of the top layer of cake with a little syrup before placing on top.

Decorate the top of the cake with rosettes of whipped cream around the edges and pile the whole, wiped strawberries and fraise des bois in the centre. Dust with icing sugar and refrigerate until ready to serve. This cake will keep well overnight in the refrigerator.

Serves 10–12

FOUR MELON AND GINGER SALAD

*D*uring the summer months melons are abundant. Mostly imported from France, Italy and Spain, they are wonderfully juicy and refreshing. I have selected four different types to combine a variety of colours and flavours. There are so many different ones you need not be restricted by my choice. The ginger syrup was inspired by reading Bridget Allen's book Cooking with Garlic, Ginger and Chillies. Mine is a little less pungent than the original recipe in order to allow the taste of the melons to come through.

INGREDIENTS

25 g (1 oz) root ginger
100 g (3¾ oz) demerara sugar
275 ml (10 fl oz) water
4 small melons eg Ogen,
  water melon, cantaloupe,
  honeydew

large tub Greek yoghurt

METHOD

Grate the ginger into a small pan. Use a pastry brush dipped in a little of the water to brush down the grater and release all the bits. Add the sugar and water to the pan and cook slowly to dissolve the sugar. Bring to the boil and simmer fairly fast, keeping a watchful eye on the mixture for 10–15 minutes until it has reduced by half and become thick and syrupy. Pass through a fine sieve and chill.

Cut the melons into sections and remove the skin and seeds. Cut into smaller wedges or slices and arrange a few of each variety on dessert plates or one large platter. Spoon over the ginger syrup and serve with yoghurt.

Serves 8–10

WATER MELON CRUSH

*T*here are several varieties of water melon. For this recipe I prefer to use the dark and light green stripy 'Tiger' melon. It has a deep pink flesh, a sweet flavour and fewer pips than many of the other varieties. One of the most important factors is that your melon be fully ripe when you buy it. Once picked, melons do not improve in flavour. A crush, or granita as it is often known, differs from a sorbet or water ice in that it contains less sugar and rather than yielding a smooth frozen texture, it forms a mass of jewel-like crystals.

INGREDIENTS

125 g (4½ oz) caster sugar
250 ml (9 fl oz) water

1 kg (2 lb 2 oz) water melon flesh (a 2 kg (4 lb 4 oz) melon yields approx 1 kg (2 lb 2 oz) flesh)
juice of 1 lemon

METHOD

Combine the sugar and water in a small pan and heat gently to dissolve the sugar. Increase the heat and boil for 2 minutes. Remove from the heat and cool.

Cut the melon into wedges, remove and discard the skin. Roughly cube the flesh, prising out the pips as you go. I find the handle of a teaspoon is a useful gadget for this.

In a food processor or liquidiser mix the melon cubes with the sugar syrup and process to a smooth purée. Add lemon juice to taste.

Pour the purée into a shallow container and freeze for 45 minutes to 1 hour. During this time ice crystals will start to form around the edges of the container. Remove the granita from the freezer and break up the crystals with a fork using a stirring and scraping action. Return to the freezer and repeat every 45 minutes until you have a glistening mass of crystals. This can take 2–3 hours. Cover the container and freeze until required.

Serve, within 1 to 2 days of making, in tall glasses with long spoons. Alternatively, if you cut your melon in half before scooping out the flesh, the half shell can be used as a serving container.

Serves 8

AUTUMN

Autumn is harvest time and orchards everywhere are bursting with glorious fruit. This has to be my favourite season with endless varieties to choose from. As the leaves begin to turn so apples, pears, plums and quinces ripen. Each year I find myself full of anticipation as I wait to pick the fruit from my own trees. Blackberries are in profusion on our hedgerows and figs are in their prime. All these fruits teamed with spices, honey, toffee and caramel make autumn a cook's paradise.

LEFT: *Blackberries and Mulberries with Lemon Grass Scented Cheese*

BLACKBERRIES AND MULBERRIES WITH LEMON GRASS SCENTED CHEESE

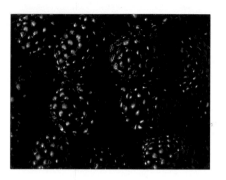

If you are short of time or if lemon grass is unavailable you can omit the first stage, using a little extra lemon zest and juice to flavour the cheese at the second stage. Personally I prefer to use the lemon grass as it has a slightly more fragrant, subtle taste with a hint of the exotic. Serve this dessert with a sweet almond biscuit.

Mulberries have an unusual flavour and are a most welcome autumn berry. They can be quite tart and require a lot of sweetening.

INGREDIENTS

2 stalks lemon grass
50 g (2 oz) caster sugar
150 ml (5 fl oz) crème fraîche
450 g (1 lb) curd cheese
juice of ½ lemon

200 g (7 oz) raspberries
50 g (2 oz) icing sugar
juice of ½ lemon

110 g (4 oz) blackberries
110 g (4 oz) mulberries
  or raspberries
icing sugar

sweet almond biscuits

METHOD

Two days before you want to serve the dessert, halve the lemon grass lengthwise then bash it with the heel of a large knife to release the juices. Chop roughly, then add to the caster sugar and crème fraîche. Stir to combine, cover and chill for 24 hours.

The day before serving, press the curd cheese through a sieve into a bowl. Pass the scented crème fraîche through the same sieve and discard the lemon grass. Stir into the cheese until smooth. Add a little lemon juice to taste.

Cut twelve pieces of damp muslin into 20 cm (8 in) squares. Lay out six pieces on a clean work surface and lay the remaining six on top to give a double layer.

Divide the cheese mixture between the six squares, spooning it into the centre. Gather up the corners of each cloth and tie together to form a ball. Using string hang the cheeses from a refrigerator shelf and slide a tray just below to catch the drips. Leave for 24 hours. It may be necessary to tighten the cloths once or twice during this process.

Press the raspberries through a sieve and discard the pips. Add the icing sugar and lemon juice to taste.

Pour a little raspberry sauce onto each of six dessert plates. Remove the cheese from the muslin cloths and stand one on each plate. Add a few whole mixed blackberries and mulberries, dust with a little icing sugar and serve with sweet-almond biscuits.

Serves 6

WALNUT BREAD AND BUTTER PUDDING WITH BLACKBERRIES

I like to make this homely pudding using the walnut and raisin bread on page 100. Rather than shaping it into a flat bread, place it in a 450 g (1 lb) loaf tin and bake for 25–30 minutes until well risen and golden. Allow it to cool before slicing. Obviously a commercial walnut loaf is a good alternative if time is short. If blackberries are not available ring the changes with blueberries or raspberries. Have plenty of the fruits so that there is no danger of creating a slightly dry pudding.

INGREDIENTS

50 g (2 oz) butter, softened
9 small slices walnut bread
200 g (7 oz) blackberries
4 eggs
250 ml (9 fl oz) milk
450 ml (16 fl oz) whipping
  cream
180 g (6 oz) caster sugar
seeds from 1 vanilla pod

single cream to serve,
  if desired

METHOD

Butter a large, approximately 1.5 litre (2½ pint) ovenproof dish from which it is suitable to serve.

Generously butter the bread. Cut the slices in half across the diagonal and arrange them neatly overlapping in the prepared dish, buttered side uppermost.

Scatter the blackberries over the bread, tucking a few between each slice.

Beat the eggs together, then mix well with the milk, cream and sugar. Flavour with the vanilla seeds, then pour over the bread. Leave to stand for 20–30 minutes before baking to allow the bread to absorb some of the moisture.

Preheat the oven to 170°C (325°F, Gas 3, 150 Circotherm). Stand the oven-proof dish in a large roasting tray. Pour in enough hot water to come halfway up the sides of the dish and bake for 45–50 minutes. The custard should be golden and just set with crispy bits of bread showing through.

Serve warm with single cream if desired.

Serves 6

TREACLE PEAR PUDDING

If you prefer the topping of your pudding to be sticky rather than syrupy, add a couple of tablespoons of fresh breadcrumbs on top of the golden syrup before adding the fruit. This absorbs some of the liquid and gives a more traditional treacle pudding texture. If you like, warm a little extra golden syrup to pour over just before serving; alternatively, serve with cream or cinnamon custard. This makes a deliciously comforting and warming dessert on an autumnal day.

INGREDIENTS

25 g (1 oz) butter
2 heaped tablespoons
   golden syrup
1 pear

150 g (5 oz) butter, softened
150 g (5 oz) caster sugar
2 eggs, beaten
150 g (5 oz) self-raising flour
3 tablespoons cider or Perry

single cream or cinnamon
   custard (page 126)

METHOD

Use a little of the butter to grease a 1.2 litre (2 pint) pudding basin. Spoon the golden syrup into the base of the bowl. Peel, core and dice the pear and place on top of the syrup. Dot with the remaining butter.

Cream the butter and sugar until light and fluffy. Incorporate the eggs little by little, beating well between each addition. Sift the flour and fold in, adding enough cider to give a firm dropping consistency.

Spoon the mixture into the pudding basin on top of the fruit. Cover with a disc of buttered greaseproof paper.

Cut a circle of foil that will overhang the top of the basin by 7.5 cm (3 in). Make a 1 cm (½ in) pleat in the foil then place it over the basin and tie securely with string. The pleat allows for expansion during cooking. I find it useful to leave the string long and use the excess to form a handle or loop which makes lifting the pudding easier.

Stand the basin on a trivet in a deep pan. Add enough water to come 5 cm (2 in) up the sides of the bowl. Cover with a tightly fitting lid and steam for 1–1½ hours. To test if the pudding is cooked, remove the foil and greaseproof paper disc and insert a small skewer into the centre; it should come out clean. If not cooked, re-cover the basin and steam for a little longer. If cooked ahead of time, turn off the heat and leave until required.

Lift the pudding from the pan, snip the string and remove the foil and the greaseproof paper disc. Invert the basin onto a serving dish. Serve with single cream or cinnamon custard.

Serves 6

AUTUMN PUDDING

This dessert is based on the traditional summer pudding recipe, but here I use a classic autumn combination of apples and black-berries. Although the ingredients call for cooking apples, many varieties of eating apples could easily be substituted. You may need to adjust the quantity of sugar to suit both the fruits and your tooth.

INGREDIENTS

500 g (1 lb 2 oz) cooking apples
180 g (6 oz) caster sugar
juice of ½ lemon
500 g (1 lb 2 oz) blackberries
11 slices stale white bread, medium sliced, crusts removed

single cream

METHOD

Peel and core the apples and cut into wedges. Place in a large heavy based saucepan with the sugar and lemon juice. Cover and cook over a medium heat for 5–10 minutes, until the apple slices are soft but retain their shape. Add the blackberries, stirring once only and cook for a further 2–3 minutes. Remove from the heat and set on one side.

Reserve one or two slices of bread for the top and line a 1.2 litre (2 pint) pudding basin with the remainder. Overlap the slices slightly and ensure there are no gaps.

Spoon the cooked fruits and a good amount of the juice into the lined basin. Top with the reserved bread slices. Place a small plate or saucer on top of the pudding and stand a medium-sized can from your store cupboard on top to act as a weight. Refrigerate overnight. Strain and reserve the remaining juices in the refrigerator.

When ready to serve, remove the weight and the plate from the pudding and invert the basin onto your serving dish. Holding both the dish and the pudding basin securely give a sharp jolt and the pudding will slide out. Pour the reserved juice over the bread to give it a lovely rich blackberry colour and serve with single cream.

Serves 6

POACHED QUINCES WITH BRIE

*S*omewhere between a dessert and a cheese course, this is a wonderful way to end a meal. Originating from Central Asia, quinces belong to the same family as the apple and the pear. They are large golden-yellow fruits, hard even when ripe and often covered in down. Their autumnal fragrance is one of life's great pleasures. They always require cooking and here, simply poached in a light wine syrup, they take on a pinkish golden glow. Choose a piece of fully ripe Brie and keep it at room temperature so as not to mar its flavour and texture.

INGREDIENTS

2 large or 4 small quinces
570 ml (1 pint) dry white wine
125 g (4½ oz) granulated sugar

175 g (6 oz) strong white
   plain flour
175 g (6 oz) wholemeal flour
1 teaspoon salt
1½ generous teaspoons easy
   blend dried yeast
25 g (1 oz) soft light
   brown sugar
25 g (1 oz) walnuts, chopped
50 g (2 oz) raisins
200 ml (7 fl oz) warm milk
2 tablespoons olive oil

450 g (1 lb) ripe Brie

METHOD

Peel, core and slice the quinces and place in a pan with the wine and granulated sugar. The liquid should just cover the fruit. Simmer very slowly over a low heat for 1–1½ hours or until the slices are tender and the wine is reduced and syrupy. It will be necessary to turn the slices from time to time. Cool.

To make the bread place the flours and salt into a large mixing bowl. Stir in the yeast and light brown sugar. Add the walnuts and raisins. Make a well in the centre and pour in the warmed milk and olive oil. Stir, gradually incorporating the flour until the mixture starts to form a dough. Continue working using your hands at this stage until all the ingredients are combined and the dough leaves the sides of the bowl clean. Transfer to a lightly floured surface and knead for 5–7 minutes until the dough is smooth and elastic.

Return the dough to the cleaned out bowl, cover with clingfilm and leave in a warm, but not hot, place until doubled in volume. This will take 1–2 hours depending on the temperature. Do not rush the process or you will spoil the texture of the bread.

Knock back the dough and knead again for 1–2 minutes. Shape into a large oblong 32 x 18 cm (13 x 7 in) and place on a lightly greased baking sheet. Cover with a clean tea towel and prove in a warm place for 15–20 minutes.

Preheat the oven to 230°C (450°F, Gas 8, 190 Circotherm). Bake the bread for 20–25 minutes until risen and golden. Let it cool on a wire rack.

With a long serrated bread knife cut vertically through the bread at regular intervals to give sixteen sticks 2 cm wide x 18 cm long (¾ in x 7 in). Place on a large baking tray and warm for 5 minutes in a low oven before serving with the quinces and a slice of Brie.

Serves 8

PEARS IN PERRY

Autumn wouldn't be the same without at least one dessert of poached pears. Here I have cooked them with aniseed and lemon grass for a slightly exotic flavour. If you dislike aniseed, add a split vanilla pod instead. Perry is like cider but is made from pears instead of apples. It is available from many off-licences and supermarkets. If you are unable to find Perry use a medium dry cider. It is impossible to give an exact cooking time when it comes to poaching fruit as there are so many variables. Use my time as a guide only. Bear in mind that the pears should be cooked extremely slowly. This way they will hold their shape and absorb the flavours and juices right through to the core.

INGREDIENTS

**6 firm pears (Williams,
    Packham or Rocha)
juice of I lemon
I litre (I ¾ pints) Perry
150 g (5 oz) soft brown sugar
½ star anise
I stalk lemon grass**

250 g (9 oz) marscapone

METHOD

Carefully peel the pears, keeping their shape as even as possible. Leave the stalks intact. Rub the flesh with a little lemon juice to prevent discolouration.

Place the Perry in a deep pan large enough to take all the pears. Stir in the sugar and heat gently until dissolved. Add the anise and lemon grass, cut in half lengthwise and then into two or three pieces. Add any remaining lemon juice.

Bring the syrup to the boil. Gently lower the pears into the syrup making sure they are submerged in the liquid. Cover with a disc of greaseproof paper and a tightly fitting lid. Simmer very gently for I ¼ hours or until tender.

The pears will have taken on the wonderful golden colour of the syrup and become almost translucent. Insert a skewer or small knife into one of the pears to ensure it is soft right through to the centre.

Remove the greaseproof paper and, using a slotted spoon, transfer the pears to a serving bowl. Remove the star anise and lemon grass and discard. Bring the syrup to a rolling boil and cook for 10 minutes or until it lightly coats the back of a spoon. Allow to cool slightly before pouring over the pears.

Serve the pears warm or chilled with one spoonful of marscapone per person. This dish will keep for two to three days in a cool place or refrigerator.

Serves 6

BLACK GRAPE JELLIES

These jellies were invented in honour of my parents who have an extremely productive Black Hamburg grape vine, often yielding hundreds of bunches of grapes. As much as I enjoy drinking grape juice there comes a point when you need to find some alternatives. These jellies may require more or less sugar depending on the grape variety you use. I think you will agree they make a delicious pudding; also healthy! Grape juice can be made by pushing grapes through a mouli or sieve. The juice can then be diluted with a little water as required. Sweeten according to taste.

INGREDIENTS

1½ sachets (16.5 g/0.6 oz)
   gelatine
3 tablespoons water

1 kg (2 lb 2 oz) black grapes,
   seedless if possible
100 ml (3¾ fl oz) red wine
75 g (3 oz) caster sugar

6 vine leaves
extra grapes to decorate
200 ml (7 fl oz) single cream

METHOD

Soak the gelatine in the water and set aside.

Wash the grapes, deseed if necessary and place in a liquidiser or food processor. Blend until smooth. Pass through a sieve into a measuring jug; you should have approximately 700 ml (23 fl oz) of liquid.

Heat the red wine and sugar until the sugar has dissolved. Increase the heat and boil for 2 minutes. Add the soaked gelatine and stir until completely dissolved. Pour a little of the grape juice onto the wine, stir to blend, then return to the jug and stir again.

Pour into six 150 ml (5 fl oz) dariole moulds or ramekins and refrigerate for 4 hours or until set.

Lay a vine leaf on each dessert plate. Unmould the jellies by running the point of a sharp knife around the top edge. Dip each mould briefly into a basin of hot water and invert one jelly over each vine leaf.

Decorate with a few whole grapes and serve with single cream.

Serves 6

PUMPKIN AND RICOTTA TORTE WITH PINE NUTS

This torte is somewhere between an Italian ricotta cake and an American pumpkin pie. The pumpkin flavour can be enhanced by the addition of a little nutmeg if desired. I prefer to make this the day before eating. If possible, keep it overnight in a cold larder rather than a fridge which tends to make the pastry soggy. The combination of ricotta and rich orange pumpkin flesh makes a particularly pleasing and tasty mixture. The pine nuts add a crunchiness.

INGREDIENTS

450 g (1 lb) slice of pumpkin
3 tablespoons water

300 g (11 oz) pâte sucrée
  (page 170)

500 g (1 lb 2 oz) ricotta cheese
100 ml (3 fl oz) sour cream
3 eggs
200 g (7 oz) caster sugar
1 rounded tablespoon flour
50 g (2 oz) pine nuts

icing sugar

METHOD

Preheat the oven to 180°C (350°F, Gas 4, 160 Circotherm). Remove the seeds and stringy centre from your slice of pumpkin, then cut into wedges. Place them in a roasting tin with 3 tablespoons of water, cover with a sheet of kitchen foil and bake for 1–1½ hours until completely tender. Cool, then remove the skin and process the flesh in a food processor until smooth.

Grease the sides of a 22 cm (8½ in) springform tin. This will help to hold the pastry in place. Use three-quarters of the pastry to line the prepared tin, pressing the dough well into the base and sides. Chill. Roll the remaining pastry to form a rectangle and cut into long strips about 1 cm (½ in) wide. Lay on a tray and chill whilst preparing the filling.

In a large bowl beat together the ricotta cheese and the pumpkin purée until smooth. Stir in the sour cream. Beat the eggs, then add to the purée mixture with the caster sugar and flour. Blend well together. Pour or spoon into the pastry case and sprinkle the pine nuts over the top.

Brush the pastry edge with a little water or egg white, then lay the chilled strips of pastry over the torte in a lattice pattern. Trim off the ends and bake for 45–55 minutes. The filling will rise and the crust will have a gorgeous golden colour. Switch off the oven and leave the torte to cool inside.

Remove from the tin and dust with icing sugar.

Serves 8

HAZELNUT PANCAKES WITH CARAMELISED PEARS AND CHOCOLATE SAUCE

Pancakes can be made ahead of time and frozen if they are layered between squares of greaseproof paper to prevent them sticking. Place them in a plastic bag so they are airtight. Be sure to defrost them in plenty of time and warm them through before serving. Equally they can be refrigerated for 2 days. The joy of this pudding is to serve everything hot and let the ice cream or cream melt into the fruit and chocolate sauce.

INGREDIENTS

75 g (3 oz) plain flour
50 g (2 oz) ground hazelnuts
1 dessertspoon caster sugar
1 whole egg
1 egg yolk
300 ml (11 fl oz) milk
25 g (1 oz) butter

110 g (4 oz) caster sugar
3 tablespoons water
110 ml (4 fl oz) water
6 pears, Conference or Williams

110 g (4 oz) chocolate
40 g (1½ oz) butter
75 ml (3 fl oz) milk

200 ml (7 fl oz) whipped cream or vanilla ice cream

METHOD

Sieve the flour into a bowl. Add the hazelnuts and sugar. Make a well in the centre and add the whole egg and egg yolk. Pour a little of the milk onto the eggs then using a whisk blend the liquids together and start drawing in the flour. Pour on the remaining milk whilst continually whisking and bringing in more and more flour. When all the milk has been added whisk really well to ensure the batter is smooth. Cover and stand at room temperature for 30 minutes.

Melt the butter in a 15 cm (6 in) non-stick frying or pancake pan, then stir it into the batter.

Ensure the pan is well greased and hot, then add a small ladleful of batter to the pan. Immediately swirl the pan around so the batter covers the base in a thin even layer. Cook over a moderate to high heat until the pancake sets and turns golden on the underside. You will have to pull a little back to check. It usually takes 30–60 seconds. Loosen the edges with a palette knife and turn the pancake over. Cook for a similar amount of time on the second side, then transfer to a plate. Make seven more pancakes in the same way and stack them on the plate, sprinkling a little sugar between each as you go. Cover with a clean tea towel until required.

Place the sugar and three tablespoons of water in a large frying pan and cook to a golden caramel. Remove from the heat. Add the remaining water to stop the cooking. Cover your hand with a cloth as you do this; the caramel is likely to spit and splutter. Return the pan to the heat and cook slowly, stirring from time to time until the caramel has dissolved.

Peel and core the pears, then cut each one into eight pieces. Add to the caramel and cook over a low heat for 10 minutes or until the pears are tender and have taken on a wonderful golden glow. The important thing here is to get the pears tender all the way through without letting them break up. They must be cooked very slowly. Keep warm.

Place the chocolate, butter and milk in a bowl and stand over a pan of gently simmering water. Do not allow the bowl to touch the water below. Leave for 5 minutes until everything is warm and soft, then stir to mix.

To serve, cover the plate of pancakes with kitchen foil and warm through in the oven for 10 minutes. Lay a pancake on each dessert plate; top with a spoonful of the warm pears. Add a generous scoop of whipped cream or vanilla ice cream (this will start to melt immediately so be sure you are absolutely ready with everything else) and drizzle over a spoonful of chocolate sauce.

Serves 8

TREACLE TART

Although not exactly an original recipe it would be hard to write a chapter on autumn puddings without including a treacle tart. To me, this epitomises this time of year. True nursery nostalgia, perfect comfort food as the days begin to shorten and there is a distinct nip in the air. Bliss!

INGREDIENTS

300 g (11 oz) pâte sucrée (page 170)

5 rounded tablespoons golden syrup
110 g (4 oz) fresh white breadcrumbs
zest and juice of ½ lemon

vanilla custard (page 95) or single cream to serve

METHOD

Preheat the oven to 190°C (375°F, Gas 5, 160 Circotherm). Use half the pastry to line a 20 cm (8 in) pie plate. Chill. Roll the remaining pastry to a large oblong, 3 mm (⅛ in) thick. Lay on a baking sheet that has been dusted with flour, and chill.

Warm the golden syrup in a small pan, just enough to make it runny. Stir in the breadcrumbs, lemon zest and juice. Spoon into the chilled pastry case. Brush the pastry edges with a little water.

Using a knife or pastry wheel, cut the pastry into six strips, each 23 cm (9 in) long by 1 cm (⅜ in) wide. Lay these in a lattice across the tart. Press them well against the sides to ensure they are stuck. Cut 4 cm (1½ in) diamonds out of the remaining pastry. Make a leaf pattern on each with a small knife and arrange decoratively around the edge of the tart. Chill for 10 minutes before baking for 25–30 minutes until the pastry is crisp and golden. Best served warm, with vanilla custard or single cream.

Serves 6

ALMOND CAKE WITH POACHED DAMSONS

Damsons are the small blue plum-like fruits found on hedgerows and in shops in the autumn. They are rather sharp and benefit from poaching. Here red wine and cinnamon complement their flavour well. The almond cake is moist and can be kept in an airtight container for a day or so if required. If you like, the cake mixture can be divided between eight buttered, 10 cm (4 in) tartlet tins and cooked for 5 minutes less. Serve each tartlet topped with the fruits and clotted cream.

INGREDIENTS

225 g (8 oz) butter, softened
225 g (8 oz) caster sugar
4 eggs
150 g (5 oz) self-raising flour
75 g (3 oz) ground almonds
2 tablespoons milk

150 g (5 oz) caster sugar
300 ml (11 fl oz) red wine
1 cinnamon stick
450 g (1 lb) damsons
1 rounded teaspoon arrowroot
1 tablespoon water

icing sugar for dusting
8 tablespoons clotted cream

METHOD

Preheat the oven to 180°C (350°F, Gas 4, 160 Circotherm). Melt a little butter and use to grease a 22 cm (8½ in) loose-bottomed cake tin.

Cream the butter and caster sugar until soft and light. This can be done with a wooden spoon or with an electric whisk. Beat the eggs together, then gradually add to the mixture, beating well between each addition. Sieve the flour and, using a metal spoon or rubber spatula, carefully fold into the batter along with the almonds and milk. Spoon the mixture into the prepared tin, spreading it out slightly. Cook for 25–30 minutes until well risen and golden. Remove the cake from the oven. Transfer to a wire rack to cool.

Combine the caster sugar, red wine and cinnamon stick in a medium pan and cook to dissolve the sugar. Halve the damsons and remove the stones. If you are using the tiny English damsons you may prefer to leave them whole – but do warn your guests. Add them to the wine syrup and poach very slowly for 4–5 minutes until they are soft but retain their shape.

With a slotted spoon, remove the cinnamon stick and fruit from the liquid and transfer to a bowl. Keep warm. Return the syrup to the heat and boil rapidly until reduced by half. Mix the arrowroot with a little cold water. Add a tablespoon of the hot syrup, then return to the pan and stir until thickened. Boil for 30 seconds; pour over the damsons.

Place a slice of cake on each plate. Dust with icing sugar. To one side spoon a little of the hot fruit and top with a spoonful of clotted cream.

Serves 8

FIGS IN BEAUJOLAIS NOUVEAU
WITH FIG ICE CREAM

When *Beaujolais Nouveau is released on the third Thursday in November the race begins to be the first to drink this new, fresh wine. Made from the Gamay grape it is light and fruity and is a delicious contrast to the richness of the figs in this recipe. The colours of this dessert are reminiscent of late autumn, all reds and purples. Although simple to make it can look quite spectacular. The fig ice cream is sublime and makes the perfect accompaniment. If time is restricted, a tub of good quality vanilla can be substituted.*

INGREDIENTS

100 g (3¾ oz) granulated sugar
3 tablespoons water
100 ml (3¾ fl oz) water
8 black figs
4 egg yolks
50 g (2 oz) caster sugar
150 ml (5 fl oz) milk
150 ml (5 fl oz) whipping
   cream
200 g (7 oz) marscapone

300 ml (11 fl oz) Beaujolais
   Nouveau
150 ml (5 fl oz) water
125 g (4½ oz) caster sugar
1 sprig rosemary
1 stick cassia or cinnamon
12 black figs

METHOD

Combine the granulated sugar and 3 tablespoons of water in a small pan. Cook over a low heat to dissolve the sugar. Brush down any grains of sugar from the sides of the pan with a pastry brush dipped in water. Increase the heat, and cook to a golden caramel. Remove from the heat and carefully add the remaining water. It will spit and splutter so protect your hand with a cloth as you do this. Return to the heat and cook slowly for 1 minute. Peel and quarter the figs and add to the caramel. Cook for 2–3 minutes until the figs are tender, then set aside to cool. Do not worry if they break up a little.

In a bowl beat the egg yolks and caster sugar until thick and pale. Pour the milk and cream into a saucepan and bring to the boil. Pour a little of the milk and cream mixture onto the yolks. Stir to blend, then return to the remaining milk in the pan. Cook, stirring over a low heat until the custard thickens just enough to coat the back of a spoon. Do not let it boil. Cool.

Combine the cooled custard with the cooked figs and marscapone. Pour into an ice cream machine and churn until thick. Transfer to a freezerproof container and freeze until required.

Place the wine, water, caster sugar, rosemary and cassia in a pan large enough to take the uncooked figs. Cook over a low heat to dissolve the sugar. Turn up the heat and boil for 2 minutes, then reduce the heat to a gentle simmer.

Prick the figs with a skewer. Place them in the syrup. Poach for 10 minutes. Using a slotted spoon, transfer the figs to a bowl. Remove the cassia and rosemary. Reduce the liquid until syrupy, then pour over the figs. Serve the figs warm or cold, two per person, accompanied by a scoop of the fig ice cream.

Serves 6

SWEET FIG FOCACCIA

Trying to use up some leftover focaccia dough, I decided to experiment with sweet toppings. Figs worked perfectly! Everyone who tasted it agreed, including those who did not particularly like figs. It was delicious. Other fruits that work well are plums and red grapes. I add a few muscatels to the grapes to intensify flavour.

INGREDIENTS

175 g (6 oz) plain flour
25 g (1 oz) caster sugar
1 teaspoon easy blend
  dried yeast
grated zest of 1 lemon
110 ml (4 fl oz) tepid water
1 dessertspoon melted butter

25 g (1 oz) ground almonds
grated zest and juice
  of 1 orange
8 black figs
25 g (1 oz) soft brown sugar

200 ml (7 fl oz) crème fraîche

METHOD

Have all the ingredients for the dough at room temperature. Sieve the flour into a large bowl. Mix in the caster sugar, yeast and the grated lemon zest. Add the water and melted butter and stir to blend. Work the mixture until it holds together adding a little more water if necessary.

Turn the dough onto a lightly floured surface and knead for 5 minutes. It will become smooth and elastic.

Shape the dough into a ball and place in the base of a large clean bowl, allowing it plenty of room to rise. Cover the bowl with clingfilm and leave in a warm place for 1½ hours or until doubled in volume. Above a radiator, in an airing cupboard or in a warm kitchen is ideal. The dough must not get too hot.

Preheat the oven to 190°C (375°F, Gas 5, 160 Circotherm). Lightly butter a large baking sheet.

Knock back the dough and knead for 2–3 minutes. Shape into a ball and roll to a circle approximately 30 cm (12 in) in diameter. Carefully transfer the dough to the baking sheet. Cover with a clean tea towel and leave to prove for 10 minutes.

Sprinkle the almonds and grated orange zest over the dough circle. Cut the figs into eighths and place randomly on top. Sprinkle with the soft brown sugar and squeeze over 1–2 teaspoons of orange juice.

Bake in the preheated oven for 20 minutes, until the focaccia is golden and the figs softened.

Serve hot or warm with a good spoonful of crème fraîche per person.

Serves 6

POACHED PLUMS WITH GINGER AND CASSIA

Plums are available in late summer and early autumn, but somehow I always associate their flavour with the autumn. The addition of cassia, the dried bark of a Chinese evergreen tree, not unlike cinnamon, gives a warm spiciness to the syrup. Plums vary enormously in size, colour and taste. For this recipe I would suggest using a variety such as Marjorie Seedling, Victoria, President or Stanley. Look for firm, plump specimens with no unsightly bruises and preferably a good bloom. Monitor the poaching process carefully as different varieties may require more or less cooking time.

INGREDIENTS

350 ml (12 fl oz) water
150 g (5 oz) soft brown sugar
450 g (1 lb) plums
2.5 cm (1 in) piece of root ginger, chopped
2 pieces cassia bark

175 ml (6 fl oz) crème fraîche

METHOD

Place the water and sugar in a large pan and bring slowly to the boil. Stir once or twice to ensure the sugar has dissolved.

Wash the plums, then cut in half and remove the stones. Add to the syrup with the chopped ginger and pieces of cassia bark. Simmer on the lowest possible heat for 7–10 minutes. The liquid should barely be moving, just one or two bubbles or the plums will turn to purée! Test with a small skewer to see if the fruit is cooked. When tender transfer to a serving bowl, using a slotted spoon. Discard the cassia bark.

Return the syrup to the heat and boil rapidly until slightly thickened. Remember it will thicken more as it cools down. Set aside to cool, then pour over the plums. Chill until required.

Serve the plums and their juices accompanied with crème fraîche. The plums will keep well in a cool place or refrigerator for a few days.

Serves 4

ROASTED FIGS
WITH CARDAMON AND ORANGE BUTTER SAUCE

Perhaps I should call these Adam and Eve Figs. Fig leaves do not have many uses but if you know someone with a tree they can be an attractive addition here. I like to use black figs; their deep red centres look particularly stunning. The skins are usually thin and are quite edible so there is no need to peel them. As figs require warm sun to ripen fully, most are imported from the Mediterranean. Choose unbruised fruit for best results.

INGREDIENTS

16 black figs
2–3 fig leaves if available
110 g (4 oz) butter
110 g (4 oz) caster sugar
zest and juice of 1 orange
6 cardamon pods, split

large tub crème fraîche

METHOD

Preheat the oven to 180°C (350°F, Gas 4, 160 Circotherm).

Stand the figs upright on their ends. Cut carefully down through the skin and flesh into quarters, only cutting halfway through to the base so that they remain intact.

Select an ovenproof dish which can double as a serving dish and is just large enough to take the fruit in a single layer. Lay the fig leaves on the bottom, allowing them to come up the sides if desired. Arrange the figs on top.

Melt the butter in a small pan. Add the sugar, orange zest and juice and the split cardamon pods; spoon over the figs.

Cook in the preheated oven for 15–20 minutes, basting frequently until soft and beginning to caramelise.

Cool slightly before serving straight from the dish with lashings of crème fraîche.
Serves 8

PIP'S PLUM CAKE

The recipe for this delicious yeasted plum cake was given to me by Pip Koppel. She recommends using the blue Polish plums that are sometimes available in our shops. These were unavailable when I was testing it so I substituted Wyedale cooking plums. The cake looked and tasted fantastic. The wonderful pink juices just began to run and moisten the dough below. You may omit the crumble topping. Simply butter a piece of grease-proof paper and lay it over the plums for the first 20 minutes or so, then remove it and sprinkle the fruit with a little sugar and perhaps a pinch of cinnamon. Cook for 5–10 minutes more.

INGREDIENTS

250 g (9 oz) strong white plain flour
½ teaspoon salt
1 teaspoon caster sugar
½ a 7 g sachet of easy blend dried yeast
125 ml (4½ fl oz) water
1 small egg, beaten
50 g (2 oz) butter, melted

50 g (2 oz) plain flour
40 g (1½ oz) caster sugar
40 g (1½ oz) butter

500 g (1 lb 2 oz) plums

METHOD

Sieve the strong flour with the salt and sugar into a large bowl. Add the dried yeast and stir to disperse it evenly through the flour. Make a well in the centre.

Heat the water until it is tepid and combine with the egg and melted butter. Pour into the flour well and, stirring with a wooden spoon, gradually incorporate the flour until a smooth dough is formed. Turn onto a lightly floured surface and knead for 5–8 minutes until smooth and elastic. This may be done in an electric mixer using a dough hook. Return the dough to the bowl, cover with a clean tea towel and leave in a warm place for 1 hour or until doubled in size.

Preheat the oven to 190°C (375°F, Gas 5, 160 Circotherm). Grease a large baking tray. Sieve the plain flour into a bowl and add the sugar. Cut the butter into small pieces, then add to the bowl; working lightly, rub the mixture between your fingers and thumbs to make a coarse crumble. Set aside.

Knock back the dough and turn onto a lightly floured surface. Knead for 1 minute then press or roll into a 28 cm (11 in) circle. Part of the beauty of this circle is its slightly free-form shape so do not make it too regular. Alternatively make it into a rough rectangle. Place on the baking tray, cover and leave to prove for 10 minutes.

Halve and stone the plums, place skin-side down on the dough. Sprinkle over the crumble mixture, and bake for 25–30 minutes until the dough is firm and risen, the crumble is golden and crisp and the juices are just beginning to run from the plums.

This is delicious hot or cold, but it does not keep well as the base absorbs the juices and becomes soggy.

Serves 6–8

YELLOW PLUMS SET IN SAUTERNES JELLY

The tiny French mirabelle plums have the most delicious flavour and are well worth buying if you ever spot them. They are available from late summer to early autumn. These combined with the early Pershore Yellow Egg would work well here. Alternatively use Victorias or Santa Rose – not strictly yellow but the flesh cooks to a yellowy orange. Sauternes is expensive but a little goes a long way and the flavour is all important. Do not try to substitute a cheap sweet wine as you will only end up with a disappointing result.

INGREDIENTS

1 sachet (11 g/0.4 oz) and
** 1 teaspoon gelatine**
2 tablespoons water

400 ml (14 fl oz) Sauternes
200 ml (7 fl oz) water
50 g (2 oz) granulated sugar
700 g (1½ lb) yellow plums
** (½ Victoria, ½ Mirabelles)**

single cream

METHOD

Soak the gelatine in the water in a small bowl.

Combine the Sauternes with the water and sugar in a pan large enough to take all the fruit. Cook over a low heat to dissolve the sugar. Bring to the boil.

Halve the plums and remove the stones. Add the Victoria plums to the syrup and poach gently for 4–5 minutes. Add the Mirabelles and poach for two more minutes. They should be tender but retain their shape.

With a slotted spoon carefully transfer the plums to a 1.2 litre (2 pint) mould or glass serving bowl.

Add the soaked gelatine to the liquid in the pan and stir to dissolve.

Pass through a sieve lined with a square of damp muslin, then pour over the fruits. Cool and refrigerate until set.

Unmould onto a serving plate or serve from the bowl with single cream.

Serves 8

PLUM SUEDOISE

*T*here are so many varieties of plums, I feel it is best not to be too specific about which to use. If you grow your own you will want to use up whatever you have. I have made this recipe using Majorie Seedlings, Ponds Seedlings and Burbanks. The best advice is to use full-flavoured fruit and adjust the amount of sugar you add according to their sweetness. I first made a suédoise when I was at the Cordon Bleu school in London. It is one of those recipes that I have enjoyed making ever since. Its light, refreshing fruitiness must be good for you!

INGREDIENTS

1½ sachets (16.5 g/0.6 oz)
   gelatine
4 tablespoons water

250 g (9 oz) caster sugar
570 ml (1 pint) water
1 kg (2 lb 2 oz) plums

single cream

METHOD

Sprinkle the gelatine onto the water in a small pan. Leave to soak.

Combine the sugar and water in a pan large enough to take all the fruit. Cook over a low heat to dissolve the sugar.

Halve and stone the plums and poach in the sugar syrup over a very low heat for 7–10 minutes. Even when fully ripe the fruit must be allowed to cook through. This enables the syrup to soak in and prevents discolouration.

With a slotted spoon lift out 12 plum halves. Drain them well and place in a circle around the base of a 20 cm (8 in), 1.2 litre (2 pint) cake tin or charlotte mould. Remember the bottom will be the top when the dessert is turned out. It is personal preference that dictates whether you place them skin side up or down.

Drain the remaining fruit, reserving the syrup. Pass the plums through a sieve. You should end up with approximately 450 ml (16 fl oz) of fruit purée. Mix this with enough of the syrup to make up to 850 ml (1½ pints).

Heat the gelatine over a very low heat to dissolve it. Do not allow it to get too hot or it will become stringy. Stir into the fruit purée until well blended. Allow to cool, then carefully pour the purée over the plums in the tin. If the plums begin to move as you do this it may be easiest to pour in a thin layer of jelly and allow this to set around the plums before topping up with the remainder. Leave to set in the fridge.

Run the point of a small knife around the top edge of the suédoise, then dip the mould briefly into a basin of hot water. Invert onto your serving dish, give one good shake and the dessert will slide out. Serve with single cream.

Serves 6–8

ORANGE WAFERS WITH
PAN-FRIED APPLES AND ORANGES

Both the custard and the wafers can be made a day or two before serving. The custard can be kept covered in the fridge and the biscuits stored in an airtight container. The apples can be cooked in advance and either reheated or kept warm in a low oven. This leaves only the assembling to do just before serving.

INGREDIENTS

60 g (2½ oz) butter
1 tablespoon golden syrup
60 g (2½ oz) caster sugar
zest and juice of ½ orange
40 g (1½ oz) ground almonds
30 g (1¼ oz) plain flour

250 ml (9 fl oz) milk
1 vanilla pod, split
3 egg yolks
60 g (2½ oz) caster sugar

4 oranges
5 dessert apples
110 g (4 oz) caster sugar
3 tablespoons water
50 g (2 oz) butter

METHOD

Preheat the oven to 180°C (350°F, Gas 4, 160 Circotherm). Grease two large baking sheets. In a small pan combine the butter, syrup and sugar with the orange zest and juice. Cook over a low heat until the butter has melted and the sugar dissolved. Remove from the heat and stir in the almonds and flour.

Place spoonfuls of the mixture, spaced at least 15 cm (6 in) apart, onto the baking trays. Bake for 7–8 minutes until bubbling and golden. You should have enough mixture to make twelve biscuits.

Allow the biscuits to cool for 30 seconds before using a palette knife to transfer them to a wire rack. When cold, store in an airtight container until needed.

Pour the milk into a small pan with the split vanilla pod. Place over the heat and bring to the boil. In a bowl whisk together the egg yolks and sugar until thick and pale. Pour a little of the boiling milk onto the yolks, stir to blend, then return to the milk pan. Cook slowly whilst continually stirring until the custard thickens to coat the back of the spoon. Do not allow it to boil or it will curdle. Transfer to a jug. This crème anglaise may be served warm or cold.

Use a small knife to peel the skin and pith from the oranges, then remove the segments by cutting down either side of the membranes. Set aside.
Cut the apples into quarters and remove the cores. Peel them if you prefer. Cut each quarter in half. Place the sugar and water in a large sauté or frying pan. Cook slowly to dissolve the sugar. Increase the heat and cook to a golden caramel. Plunge the base of the pan into a bowl of cold water to stop the cooking. It will sizzle and hiss briefly. Over a low heat, add the butter to the pan and stir to blend. Don't worry, it will be quite sticky to start with. Add the apples and cook until soft and coated in the caramel, 10–12 minutes Strain any juice from the oranges before adding them to the pan.

Place a wafer on each plate, top with a spoonful of the apples and oranges and finish with another wafer. Pour round a little of the crème anglaise.

Serves 6

BAKED APPLE AND CALVADOS SOUFFLES

Although a little last-minute whisking is required the apples can be hollowed out and the purée made in advance. Warm the purée through as you begin whisking the egg whites. These apple cup soufflés, like all soufflés, must be served as soon as they are cooked. The delicious thing here is not only do they look very autumnal, but your guests get to eat the apple containers, giving twice as much flavour. Calvados is a French apple brandy which really emphasises the taste of the fruits.

INGREDIENTS

8 large cooking apples
juice of 1 lemon
1 tablespoon Calvados
  or brandy
40 g (1½ oz) caster sugar
20 g (¾ oz) butter

6 teaspoons caster sugar
pinch of cinnamon

3 egg whites
25 g (1 oz) caster sugar

icing sugar

METHOD

Preheat the oven to 180°C (350°F, Gas 4, 160 Circotherm).

Choose the six best looking apples and set on one side. Peel, core and slice the remainder. Place in a small pan with half the lemon juice, the Calvados and caster sugar.

Cut a slice off the top of each of the whole apples. Using a small knife and a teaspoon scoop the flesh and core from the centre of the fruits leaving a 3 mm (⅛ in) thick wall around the base and sides. You will now have six apple cups. Brush the flesh with a little lemon juice to prevent discolouration.

Discard the pips and core from the scooped out flesh. Add any flesh to the fruit in the pan. Ensure the hollowed out apples stand upright; if not, take a thin sliver from the base. Stand spaced apart on a baking tray. Place a nob of butter in each apple cup.

Mix the caster sugar and cinnamon and rub a teaspoonful around the inside of each apple. Place the pan of apple over a low heat, cover and cook for 10 minutes until the fruit is soft and pulpy. You should end up with approximately 300 g (11 oz) purée. Keep warm.

Whisk the egg whites to stiff peaks, add the caster sugar and continue whisking until thick and glossy. Stir a spoonful of this mixture into the apple purée to loosen it. Fold in the remainder. Divide the mixture between the apple cups, filling each one right to the top.

Cook the apples in the preheated oven for 15 minutes until well risen. If using a fan oven turn the soufflés round halfway through cooking. Remove from the oven, dust the tops with a little icing sugar and serve immediately.

Serves 6

APPLE AND BLACKBERRY STRUDEL WITH CINNAMON CREAM

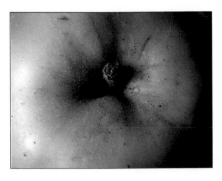

If possible, choose an apple that holds its shape during baking; Sturmer Pippins or Howgate Wonder fit the bill well. The famous Bramley is a delicious apple but tends to break down during cooking and is best reserved for purées. If time allows, gather your own blackberries from the hedgerow; I find them sweeter and more full flavoured than many of the shop-bought varieties. Remember they do not keep well and are best eaten within a day or two of picking.

INGREDIENTS

100 g (3¾ oz) fresh white breadcrumbs
50 g (2 oz) butter
4 crisp apples
150 g (5 oz) blackberries
110–150 g (4–5 oz) caster sugar
1 packet filo pastry, 6 sheets
40 g (1½ oz) butter

icing sugar

250 ml (9 fl oz) whipping cream
½ teaspoon ground cinnamon

METHOD

Preheat the oven to 180°C (350°F, Gas 4, 160 Circotherm). Grease a large baking tray.

Fry the breadcrumbs in the butter until crisp and golden Peel, core and thickly slice the apples. Mix with the blackberries and caster sugar.

Lay a clean tea towel on the work surface and dust it with flour. Lay two sheets of filo pastry, slightly overlapping, on top. This will give an oblong approximately 48 x 40 cm (19 x 16 in). Sprinkle with half the breadcrumbs, then lay two more sheets of filo on top. Sprinkle with the remaining crumbs and finally top with the last two sheets of filo. Leaving a 5 cm (2 in) border all round, spoon the fruit filling evenly over the dough.

Using the tea towel to help you, roll the pastry and filling away from you like a swiss roll. You should now end up with a roll 48 cm (19 in) long by approximately 10 cm (4 in) in diameter. Slide it carefully onto the baking tray. Melt the remaining butter and brush liberally over the top and sides of the strudel.

Bake for 35–40 minutes until golden and crisp. Dust with icing sugar. Serve hot or warm with whipped cream flavoured with a little cinnamon.

Serves 8

TOFFEED APPLE AND PECAN TART

This tart tastes best if made on the day of serving, but well in advance giving you time to chill it in the refrigerator for at least 3 hours. This firms up the filling giving a toffee-like quality. I like to use a crisp dessert apple such as a Granny Smith or russet with plenty of flavour that will retain its shape during cooking. This dessert makes the quintessential ending to a Thanksgiving dinner.

INGREDIENTS

200 g (7 oz) pâte sucrée
  (page 170)

2 small eggs, beaten
150 g (5 oz) butter
150 g (5 oz) light brown sugar
75 ml (3 fl oz) double cream
150 g (5 oz) pecan nuts
2 small dessert apples

200 ml (7 fl oz) double cream

METHOD

Preheat the oven to 180°C (350°F, Gas 4, 160 Circotherm).

Roll out the pastry and use to line a 23 cm (9 in) fluted tart tin. Bake blind (page 171). Use a little of the beaten egg to brush the tart case. Cook for 1 minute, then brush again and cook for a further minute.

Place the butter, sugar and cream in a pan large enough to take all the filling ingredients. Cook slowly to dissolve the sugar, bring to the boil and cook, stirring, for 1 minute. Remove from the heat and stir in the pecan nuts. Allow to cool slightly.

Peel and core the apples and cut into 1 cm (½ in) dice. Stir into the toffee mixture along with the beaten egg. Spoon into the prepared pastry case and bake for 20–25 minutes. Leave to cool and serve with double cream.

Serves 8

UPSIDEDOWN CIDER, APPLE AND PEAR CAKE

This moist cake with its syrupy caramelised top makes a delicious indulgent pudding when served hot. If you should be lucky enough to have any left over, it is also wonderful served cold for tea the following day. My preference is to use Williams or Packham pears and any variety of crisp eating apple.

INGREDIENTS

150 g (5 oz) caster sugar
3 tablespoons water

2 dessert apples
2 pears
25 g (1 oz) butter
2 tablespoons cider
1 tablespoon caster sugar

120 g (4½ oz) butter, softened
100 g (3¾ oz) soft light
 brown sugar
2 whole eggs
100 g (3¾ oz) self-raising flour
1 teaspoon ground cinnamon

500 ml (18 fl oz) milk
4 cinnamon sticks
6 egg yolks
120 g (4½ oz) caster sugar

METHOD

Preheat the oven to 180°C (350°F, Gas 4, 160 Circotherm). Butter a 23 cm (9 in) fixed bottom cake tin and line the base with a disc of greaseproof paper.

Place the caster sugar and water in a small pan and cook over a low heat to dissolve the sugar. Use a clean pastry brush dipped in water to wash down any grains of sugar from the sides of the pan. Turn up the heat and without stirring allow the sugar to cook to a golden caramel. Carefully pour the caramel into the base of the prepared tin. Swirl around to cover the tin evenly.

Peel and core the apples and pears. Take one apple and one pear, cut each into eight equal pieces and arrange decoratively on top of the caramel. Dot with a knob of butter and set aside. Roughly dice the remaining apple and pear and place in a small bowl with the cider and caster sugar. Set aside.

Cream the softened butter and soft light brown sugar until soft and pale. Beat the eggs together, then gradually beat into the butter. Sieve together the flour and ground cinnamon and, using a large metal spoon or rubber spatula, lightly fold into the batter mixture. Add the sliced fruit, folding it in along with the juice. Spoon this cake mixture over the diced apple and pear in the tin, level the top and bake for 45–50 minutes. Insert a skewer into the cake. If it comes out clean the cake is ready.

Cool in the tin for 2 minutes before turning onto your serving plate.

For the cinnamon custard, put the milk and cinnamon sticks into a pan and bring to the boil. Whisk the egg yolks and caster sugar together until pale and thick. Stir in a little boiling milk, then return to the remaining milk in the pan. Cook, stirring, until thickened. Do not allow the custard to boil. Discard the cinnamon. Serve the warm custard with the cake.

Serves 8

STEAMED GINGER PUDDING WITH BUTTERSCOTCH SAUCE

Although steamed puddings take quite a while to cook they are simple to prepare and once cooked can be left in the covered pan for 30–40 minutes before serving, making them trouble free. Stem ginger in syrup is available from most supermarkets and delicatessens. Originally from China it is made from the tender shoots of ginger simmered in a sugar syrup. The syrup in the jar makes a delicious addition to many desserts.

INGREDIENTS

3 pieces stem ginger in syrup
2 dessertspoons syrup
  from stem ginger jar
150 g (5 oz) butter, softened
150 g (5 oz) soft light
  brown sugar
2 eggs
150 g (5 oz) self-raising flour
2 teaspoons ground ginger
3–4 tablespoons milk

110 g (4 oz) butter
110 g (4 oz) soft light
  brown sugar
110 ml (4 fl oz) double cream

METHOD

Grease a 1.2 litre (2 pint) pudding basin. Chop the stem ginger and place into the basin along with the ginger syrup. In a large bowl cream together the butter and sugar until soft and light. This can be done using a wooden spoon or with an electric whisk. Beat the eggs together then gradually add to the butter, beating well between each addition.

Sieve the flour and ground ginger and, using a large metal spoon or rubber spatula, lightly fold it into the pudding mixture. Add enough milk to give a firm dropping consistency. Spoon the mixture into the pudding basin on top of the stem ginger. Cover with a disc of buttered greaseproof paper.

Cut a circle of foil that will overhang the top of the basin by 7.5 cm (3 in). Make a 1 cm (½ inch) pleat in the foil then place it over the basin and tie securely with string. The pleat allows for expansion during cooking. I find it useful to leave the string long and use the excess to form a handle or loop which makes lifting the pudding easier.

Stand the basin on a trivet in a deep pan. Add enough water to come 5 cm (2 in) up the sides of the bowl. Cover with a tightly fitting lid and steam for 1–1½ hours. Remove the foil and greaseproof paper disc and insert a skewer into the centre; if it comes out clean the pudding is ready. If not cooked, re-cover the basin and steam for a little longer. If your pudding has finished steaming before you are ready to eat it, turn off the heat and leave until required.

To make the sauce, place the butter, sugar and cream in a small pan and simmer gently for 1 minute.

To serve, lift the pudding from the pan, snip the string and remove the foil and greaseproof paper disc. Invert the basin onto a serving dish. Pour a little sauce over the pudding and serve the remainder separately.

Serves 6

HEDGEROW TRIFLE

Bilberries, or myrtilles as they are sometimes known, are much more popular in France than in England. If you live in an area where they grow wild you should consider yourself lucky as they are rarely sold in the shops. Those who live in urban areas will probably have to substitute blueberries. Add any other wild berries if you prefer. I like to use the large soft-centred macaroons available from most bakeries.

INGREDIENTS

3 large macaroons
4 tablespoons sherry or brandy
4 tablespoons blueberry or
blackberry jam
350 g (12 oz) fruits from the
hedgerow such as bilberries,
blackberries or wild rasp-
berries, washed and dried

250 g (9 oz) marscapone
50 g (2 oz) caster sugar
1–2 tablespoons milk

400 ml (14 fl oz) milk
1 vanilla pod, split
1 whole egg
3 egg yolks
40 g (1½ oz) caster sugar
40 g (1½ oz) plain flour

110 ml (4 fl oz)
whipping cream
a few extra berries

METHOD

Cut each macaroon into six pieces and lay in a large glass serving bowl. Spoon over the sherry or brandy. Warm the jam and spread over the macaroons. Pile the washed and dried fruits on top.

Combine the marscapone with the sugar and enough milk to give a soft consistency. Spread evenly over the fruits. Chill in the refrigerator.

Combine the milk and split vanilla pod in a saucepan and bring to the boil. Whisk the whole egg, egg yolks and sugar until thick and pale. Stir in the flour. Pour a little of the boiling milk onto the eggs, stir to blend, then return to the pan with the remainder of the milk. Cook, stirring, until the custard thickens and boiling point is reached. The flour will prevent the custard from curdling. Cook for two more minutes. Transfer to a clean bowl, dab the top with a little extra milk to prevent a skin forming, then set aside to cool. Whisk the custard to ensure it is smooth before spooning over the trifle.

Decorate with whipped cream and a few extra berries.

Serves 6

WINTER

To me winter is the most indulgent season. Filled with confections of dark, rich and smooth. This is the time to make the most of chocolate, dried fruits and nuts. The use of oranges, clementines and cranberries adds a hint of seasonal charm. As the days shorten and become colder, so the desire for hearty puddings intensifies. What could be better than a steamed orange pudding to warm you on a winter's day, or the ultimate chocolate gâteau to share with family and friends? From intimate fireside dinners to festive parties, this is the season to celebrate.

LEFT: *Orange Steamed Pudding*

ORANGE STEAMED PUDDING

Steamed puddings are one of my favourite desserts, real comfort food for cold winter days. The oranges make this one almost jewel-like in appearance and, cooked in this way, the flavour is really intense.

INGREDIENTS

150 ml (5 fl oz) water
110 g (4 oz) caster sugar
2 oranges, preferably seedless

215 g (7½ oz) butter, softened
215 g (7½ oz) caster sugar
zest of 1 orange
1½ teaspoons orange flower water
3 eggs, beaten
215 g (7½ oz) self-raising flour

freshly made custard (page 128)

METHOD

Place the water and sugar in a small pan and cook over a gentle heat to dissolve the sugar. Thinly slice the unpeeled oranges. You should get approximately six slices from each. Add to the sugar syrup ensuring they are all submerged. Cover with a disc of greaseproof paper and simmer gently for 30–40 minutes.

Lift out the orange slices with a slotted spoon or a pair of tongs and place on a wire rack over a tray to drain. Reduce the syrup by half and reserve. Butter a 1.2 litre (2 pint) pudding basin and line the base with a small disc of greaseproof paper. Place one of the orange slices on the disc and use the remainder to line the sides of the basin.

Place the softened butter and sugar in a large bowl with the orange zest. Cream together, preferably with an electric whisk, until light and fluffy. Add the orange flower water and then gradually add the beaten eggs, mixing really well between each addition. Sieve the flour and carefully fold into the batter. Spoon the pudding mixture into the lined basin. It should come three quarters of the way up the sides. Smooth the top and cover with a disc of buttered greaseproof paper. Take a large sheet of foil and fold in half to give a double thickness. Make a pleat in the centre of the foil and place over the basin. Tie with string and trim away any excess foil. The pleat will allow the pudding to expand during cooking. Leave the string long and use the excess to form a handle. This will help to remove the pudding.

Stand the basin on a trivet in a large, deep pan and add enough water to come 5 cm (2 in) up the sides. Cover with a tightly fitting lid and simmer gently for 2 hours. Check the water level from time to time. Top up as necessary. The pudding should be cooked. Remove the foil and greaseproof paper disc and insert a small skewer into the centre of the pudding. If cooked it will come out clean. If not cooked re-cover it and steam for a little longer. Simply turn out the pudding onto a warmed plate and brush with a little of the reserved syrup. Hand round a jug of freshly made custard.

This pudding can happily be made a day in advance and reheated by steaming for 35–40 minutes before serving.

Serves 6–8

MARMALADE PUMP CAKE WITH CANDIED KUMQUATS

I believe this recipe originated in Worcestershire and gained its name from the water that was pumped onto it before cooking. It has been passed between members of my family for generations. My mother serves it as a teacake filled with apricot jam. I rather like the wintry flavour of the marmalade and the addition of the compote of kumquats makes the cake more suitable for pudding. Kumquats come from Israel, Argentina and South Africa. They are tiny citrus fruits, orange in colour with a tangy flavour and an edible skin.

INGREDIENTS

125 g (4½ oz) self-raising flour
50 g (2 oz) butter, at room temperature
75 g (3 oz) caster sugar
1 egg, beaten
1 teaspoon almond essence
2 tablespoons orange marmalade
extra caster sugar for sprinkling

350 g (12 oz) kumquats
3 cloves
1 piece stem ginger in syrup, chopped
3 teaspoons ginger juice from the jar
110 ml (4 fl oz) orange juice
2–3 tablespoons soft brown sugar
2 tablespoons Cointreau or Grand Marnier

a little crème fraîche to serve if desired

METHOD

Preheat the oven to 180°C (350°F, Gas 4, 160 Circotherm). Grease an 18 cm (7 in) sandwich tin and line the base with a disc of greaseproof paper.

Sieve the flour into a bowl. Cut up the butter and rub into the flour to resemble fine breadcrumbs. Stir in the caster sugar along with the beaten egg and almond essence. Mix thoroughly with a fork until it comes together.

Spread half the mixture over the base of the prepared tin. Spoon over a layer of the marmalade, then top with the remaining cake mixture.

Turn on the cold tap to a slow to medium speed then hold the cake tin under it for a moment until thoroughly wet. Pour off the excess water and sprinkle with a little extra caster sugar. Bake for 30 minutes until risen and golden.

Remove the stems from the kumquats and cut each one in half. Remove the pips. Place in a large pan with the cloves, the chopped stem ginger, ginger juice, orange juice, soft brown sugar and liqueur. Cover the pan, bring to the boil and simmer gently for 7–10 minutes until soft.

Using a slotted spoon transfer the fruits to a serving bowl. Remove the cloves. Reduce the liquid until thick and syrupy, then pour over the fruits. Hand round with the cake and a little crème fraîche.

Serves 6

CLEMENTINE SORBET
WITH WHITE CHOCOLATE FLORENTINES

T*he florentines are a wonderful accompaniment and can be made a day or two before serving and stored in an airtight container.*

INGREDIENTS

6 clementines
200 g (7 oz) granulated sugar
200 ml (7 fl oz) water
juice of I lemon
I egg white

55 ml (2 fl oz) whipping cream
50 g (2 oz) granulated sugar
½ tablespoon golden syrup
50 g (2 oz) flaked almonds
50 g (2 oz) glacé cherries,
   chopped
25 g (I oz) mixed peel,
   chopped
25 g (I oz) plain flour
100 g (3¾ oz) white chocolate

3 clementines
I tablespoon granulated sugar

METHOD

Pare the zest from three clementines. Place in a pan with the sugar and water and bring slowly to the boil. Cook for 2 minutes, then leave to cool and infuse. Peel the remaining clementines and remove the pith from all six.

Liquidise the flesh, then pass through a strainer. Pour over the strained sugar syrup. Add a little lemon juice for flavour. Pour into an ice cream machine and churn until frozen. Whisk the egg white to soft peaks and add to the machine; churn until mixed. Transfer to a container and freeze until required.

Preheat the oven to 180°C (350°F, Gas 4, 160 Circotherm). Line two large baking sheets with baking parchment. Combine the cream, sugar and golden syrup in a pan and bring to the boil. Stir to ensure the sugar has dissolved.

Place the almonds, glacé cherries, mixed peel and flour in a bowl and pour over the cream batter. Stir to mix. Place heaped teaspoonfuls of the mixture onto the prepared trays spacing each mound well apart. Bake for 12 minutes until golden. Leave the biscuits to cool for 2 minutes and transfer to a wire rack.

Break up the white chocolate and place in a small bowl over a pan of simmering water. Keep the bowl from direct contact with the water. When the chocolate has melted spread a little onto the flat side of each biscuit. As it sets make a wiggly pattern with a fork. Leave to harden and store in an airtight container.

Pare the zest from the remaining clementines and cut into julienne strips. Place in a small saucepan with the sugar and the juice of one clementine. Heat slowly to dissolve the sugar, then bring to the boil and simmer for 4–5 minutes until the zest is cooked and begins to crystallise. Transfer to a plate to cool. If the syrup boils too quickly it will thicken and caramelise before the zests have time to cook through. If this happens add a tablespoon of water and continue cooking. Peel and divide the two remaining clementines into segments.

Take six dessert plates and place a scoop of sorbet on each. Decorate with clementine segments and a little candied zest. Place a florentine on top of each sorbet and serve immediately. Hand the remaining florentines separately.

Serves 6

ORANGES IN A CARDAMOM
AND COINTREAU SYRUP

Choose a seedless or near seedless variety of orange for this recipe. Navel oranges from the Mediterranean would be good. Do not always assume that large oranges contain more flesh; often once the skin has been peeled away you will find them dramatically reduced in size. I prefer to use Cointreau in my syrup; the slightly bittersweet flavour is a better partner to the cardamon than the very sweet Grand Marnier.

INGREDIENTS

6 seedless oranges
100 g (3¾ oz) granulated sugar
200 ml (7 fl oz) water
6 cardamom pods, split

1 tablespoon Cointreau or
Grand Marnier (optional)

50 g (2 oz) granulated sugar
2 tablespoons water

yoghurt or crème fraîche

METHOD

Pare six strips of zest from the oranges. Remove and discard any pith. Cut the zest into fine julienne strips. Blanch in boiling water for 8–10 minutes until tender. Drain and reserve.

With a sharp knife take a slice from the top and bottom of each orange. Stand an orange on either flat end and, keeping the knife as accurately as possible between the flesh and the pith, use a gentle sawing action to remove both the peel and pith. Repeat with the remaining five oranges.

Cut each orange into six slices and place in a glass serving bowl.

Cook the sugar with the water and split cardamon pods, slowly at first to dissolve the sugar. Then increase the heat and boil for 5 minutes. Pour over the oranges adding the liqueur if using. Leave to cool.

Place the remaining sugar in a small pan with the water. Cook to a golden caramel. Pour onto a lightly oiled tray and leave to cool and harden.

Just before serving break the caramel into shards by bashing it with the end of a rolling pin. Then sprinkle it, along with the reserved orange zests, over the dessert.

Serve chilled with yoghurt or crème fraîche.

Serves 6

DRIED FRUIT COMPOTE IN JASMINE TEA

There are so many dried fruits available these days that you can try this with different combinations. I like a mixture of pears, peaches, figs, apricots and sour cherries. You may find that some of the fruits soften quicker than others so spoon them into your serving bowl as they cook. Figs, for example, can take longer than other fruits. Once made, this dessert will keep for several days in a cool place and is the perfect end to a winter brunch.

INGREDIENTS

2 teaspoons jasmine tea leaves
450 g (1 lb) mixed dried fruits
zest and juice of 1 orange
1 cinnamon stick
1 tablespoon soft brown sugar

Greek yoghurt

METHOD

Spoon the tea leaves into an infuser or tie in a square of muslin. Place in a bowl and add the fruits, orange zest and cinnamon. Bring a kettle of water to the boil and pour over just enough water to cover the fruits. Leave to cool then cover and stand overnight in a cool place.

Transfer the fruits and their juices to a pan. Discard the tea leaves. Add soft brown sugar to taste and the juice of the orange. Cook over a low heat for 20–25 minutes or until the fruits are tender. Remove and discard the cinnamon stick.

Serve with spoonfuls of Greek yoghurt.

Serves 8

CRANBERRY STRUSSEL CAKE

Most cranberries come from North America, the vast bogs of New England to be precise. I have not been fortunate enough to see them being harvested, but I gather it is quite a sight. Water is flooded into the bogs, the cranberries are mechanically detached and float to form a sea of scarlet berries. Dried cranberries are now available in superkarkets; they are extremely tasty and make original additions to mixed dried fruit compôtes (page 137).

INGREDIENTS

100 g (3¾ oz) plain flour
100 g (3¾ oz) light muscovado
  sugar
1 teaspoon mixed spice
75 g (3 oz) butter, melted
50 g (2 oz) flaked almonds

100 g (3¾ oz) butter, softened
200 g (7 oz) self-raising flour
200 g (7 oz) light muscovado
  sugar
2 eggs, beaten
100 ml (3¾ fl oz) sour cream

200 g (7 oz) cranberries
zest of 1 orange
1 tablespoon light muscovado
  sugar

300 g (11 oz) cranberries
2 oranges, zest of 1,
  juice of both
75 g (3 oz) light muscovado
  sugar

icing sugar
whipped cream

METHOD

Preheat the oven to 200°C (400°F, Gas 6, 170 Circotherm). Grease a 22 cm (8½ in) springform tin and dust it with flour.

Sieve the flour, muscovado sugar and mixed spice into a mixing bowl, pour over the melted butter and mix in with a fork. You should end up with a crumbly mixture. Stir in the flaked almonds and set aside. This is the strussel topping.

Place the softened butter in a bowl, sieve in the flour and second batch of muscovado sugar, then add the eggs and sour cream. Beat with an electric whisk for 1 minute or so, until a smooth batter is formed. Spoon into the prepared tin and level the top.

Wash the cranberries and dry them well. Place them in an even layer over the cake mixture. Sprinkle the orange zest and a little muscovado sugar over the fruit. Spoon over the prepared strussel topping and bake for 30 minutes in the preheated oven. Reduce the heat to 180°C (350°F, Gas 4, 160 Circotherm) and bake for a further 30 minutes or until a skewer inserted in the centre of the cake comes out clean. The cake should be risen and golden.

Whilst the cake is cooking, prepare the compôte. Place the remaining cranberries in a pan, add the orange zest and juice and the remaining muscovado sugar. Cook slowly for 6–7 minutes until the fruits begin to pop and burst; let some remain whole. Transfer to a bowl.

Serve the cake dusted with a little icing sugar accompanied by the cranberry compote and a bowl of whipped cream.

Serves 8–10

PORT AND CRANBERRY SYLLABUB

This pretty pale pink syllabub is light and refreshing, a good choice for a Christmas party. It can be made a day or two in advance and will keep in the refrigerator without separating. Do not be tempted to substitute whipping cream as it will not support the liquid. Cranberry juice can be bought in cartons from most supermarkets. Syllabubs date back to Elizabethan times from the words sille (the area of Champagne from which the wine comes) and bub (Elizabethan for bubbling drink.)

INGREDIENTS

zest and juice of 1 lemon
75 ml (3 fl oz) cranberry juice
2 tablespoons port
60 g (2½ oz) caster sugar
300 ml (11 fl oz) double cream
grated nutmeg

METHOD

The day before serving the syllabub place the lemon zest and juice in a bowl with the cranberry juice, port and sugar. Cover and leave overnight at room temperature.

Pour the cream into a large bowl; whisk until it just begins to thicken. Add the cranberry mixture, and continue whisking to form soft peaks. Do not be tempted to whisk too fast as the cream will suddenly thicken and become overwhipped.

Spoon into six tall glasses. Grate a little nutmeg onto each. Chill until ready to serve.

Serves 6

PRUNE AND ARMAGNAC FOOL

It is said that the best prunes are those from Agen in France. This region is famous for Armagnac too so the combination is a happy one. If pruneaux d'Agen are not available, use the large ready-to-eat Californian prunes. Recently I tried some delicious vanilla-scented prunes; these would be good too. If your prunes are not of the ready-to-eat variety they may require a little soaking. Simply pour boiling water over them and leave for an hour or two before draining. The juices can be reserved and used in a meat stew or sauté.

INGREDIENTS

200 g (7 oz) prunes, pitted
2 tablespoons Armagnac
110 ml (4 fl oz) water

300 ml (11 fl oz) double cream
50 g (2 oz) icing sugar
1 tablespoon Armagnac

6 prunes, pitted
2 tablespoons Armagnac

METHOD

Place the prunes in a small pan with the Armagnac and water. Cook over a gentle heat for 10 minutes until quite soft. Pour into a liquidiser or food processor and work to a rough purée. Cool.

Whip the cream with the icing sugar and Armagnac and fold in the prune and Armagnac purée. Spoon into six small glasses. This dessert is very rich, so there is no need to be over-generous. Chill in the refrigerator until required.

Place the remaining prunes in a small bowl. Bring a kettle of water to the boil and pour over enough just to cover the prunes. Add the Armagnac and leave to cool.

Drain the prunes and serve one on top of each fool.

Serves 6

DATE CRUMBLE SLICE

Fresh dates are often sold on the branch at Middle Eastern groceries. If using fresh fruit you may like to remove the papery skins. This is easily done by cutting off the stalk end and squeezing from the opposite end. Then remove the stones and chop the flesh. The wonderful Californian Medjool dates would be delicious in this recipe. They should be stoned and chopped but require no cooking before being used in the tart. Dried dates, on the other hand, can be bought ready chopped in packets. Ensure you buy ones with no added sugar as this will make the dessert too sweet. These do require a little cooking prior to being used; follow the times below.

INGREDIENTS

125 g (4½ oz) butter, softened
50 g (2 oz) demerara sugar
I egg yolk
50 g (2 oz) ground almonds
200 g (7 oz) plain flour
250 g (9 oz) chopped dates

125 g (4½ oz) cream cheese
I teaspoon mixed spice
I tablespoon demerara sugar

icing sugar
single cream or custard

METHOD

Preheat the oven to 180°C (350°F, Gas 4, 160 Circotherm).

Prepare the dough. In a large bowl, or the bowl of a food processor, cream together the butter and demerara sugar, add the egg yolk and beat well. Fold in the ground almonds and flour. It may be necessary to work the mixture with your hands at this stage. It will look very dry but do not be tempted to add any liquid. After a short while it will easily come together into a ball. Wrap in clingfilm and chill until the dough is very firm. This will take 1–2 hours.

Place the chopped dates in a pan and cover with water. Bring to the boil and cook for 3 minutes. Turn off the heat and leave to stand for 5 minutes or until the dates are soft. Drain well.

Remove the dough from the refrigerator and cut in two. Using a coarse grater, grate half of the dough to cover the base of a 33 x 10 cm (13 x 4 in) rectangular or 23 cm (9 in) round tart tin. Press it down loosely. When cooked it will melt to form a base. Cover with an even layer of the dates. Spoon the cream cheese over the fruit and spread to cover. Grate the remaining dough over the top. Mix the spice and extra demerara sugar together, then sprinkle onto the tart. Bake for 35–40 minutes until golden brown.

Remove from the tin and dust with icing sugar before serving with single cream or custard, using the recipe on page 128.

Serves 8

BANANA TARTE TATIN

I find this variation of the classic apple tarte Tatin irresistible. The soft bananas in caramelised toffee literally melt in the mouth. For best results use firm, unblemished bananas. The tart can be made the day before serving. Simply reheat for 15 minutes in a moderate oven. At her hotel near Orleans, Caroline Tatin mistakenly put her buttered apples on to the bottom of a tart tin and then covered her mistake with a circle of pastry, since when such desserts have become ubiquitous in France.

INGREDIENTS

**150 g (5 oz) puff pastry
(page 170)**

75 g (3 oz) granulated sugar
2 tablespoons water
25 g (1 oz) butter
1 kg (2 lb 2 oz) bananas
**50 g (2 oz) soft light brown
sugar**
50 g (2 oz) butter

250 ml (9 fl oz) double cream

METHOD

Preheat the oven to 190°C (375°F, Gas 5, 160 Circotherm). Roll the puff pastry to a 25 cm (10 in) circle. Use a dinner plate as a guide. Place on a lightly floured baking sheet, prick well with a fork and chill until required.

Combine the granulated sugar and water in a small pan. Cook gently to dissolve the sugar then use a clean pastry brush dipped in a little water to brush any grains of sugar from the sides of the pan. Increase the heat and cook, without stirring, to a golden caramel. Turn off the heat and blend in the butter. Pour into the base of a 23 cm (9 in) round fixed bottom cake tin.

Peel the bananas and cut each one in half vertically. Arrange these, tightly packed, over the caramel. Sprinkle with the soft light brown sugar, then dot with butter.

Place the disc of puff pastry over the bananas, tucking in the edges to hide the fruit. Do not worry that it is slightly larger than the tin; this allows for shrinkage during cooking.

Bake for 35–40 minutes until the pastry is puffed and golden. Leave to cool in the tin for 30 minutes before turning out and serving with whipped cream.

Serves 6–8

ICED BANANA PARFAIT WITH TOFFEED BANANAS

Choose soft, ripe bananas as they will be sweet and have a full flavour. This said, do not use ones that are battered and bruised or where the flesh is discoloured as the finished parfait will also be affected. The addition of lemon juice enhances the flavour and also prevents discolouration. The parfait will keep for a few days in the freezer. Transfer it to the fridge for 30 minutes to 1 hour before serving as this will make it easier to slice. For the toffeed bananas select fruits that are ripe but firm, so that they will not break up during the cooking.

INGREDIENTS

6 egg yolks
100 g (3¾ oz) caster sugar
5 bananas
juice of ½ lemon
300 ml (11 fl oz) double cream
1 tablespoon rum (optional)

4 bananas
30 g (1¼ oz) butter
40 g (1½ oz) muscovado sugar
1 tablespoon rum (optional)
40 ml (1½ fl oz) whipping cream

METHOD

Line a 1.2 litre (2 pint) terrine or loaf tin with clingfilm and place in the freezer.

Mix the egg yolks and caster sugar in a large bowl and stand over a pan of simmering water. Do not allow the water to touch the base of the bowl. Whisk continually until thick and doubled in volume – the ribbon stage. Remove from the heat and continue whisking until cold.

Peel the bananas and mash the flesh with a little lemon juice.

Whip the cream to soft peaks. Fold the fruit and cream into the egg base. Add a little rum if desired. Pour into the terrine tin and freeze for several hours or overnight until firm.

To make the toffee bananas, cut each banana into ten diagonal slices. Melt the butter in a large frying pan. Add the muscovado sugar, and rum if desired, and cook until dissolved. Add the bananas and cook over a low to medium heat for 1 minute. Add the cream and cook for one more minute. Transfer to a plate to stop the cooking process.

Slice the terrine and serve, adding a few warm bananas and a little toffee sauce to each plate.

Serves 8

PRALINE ICE CREAM
WITH HAZELNUT FUDGE TOPPING

Praline is a combination of roasted nuts and caramel, mixed together and crushed. Here I use whole almonds but hazelnuts could be used in the same way. The ice cream can be made a day or two in advance. Transfer it to the fridge for an hour before serving to soften slightly. Served with the warm topping it becomes soft and melts in the mouth.

INGREDIENTS

50 g (2 oz) whole blanched almonds
75 g (3 oz) hazelnuts
50 g (2 oz) granulated sugar
1½ tablespoons water

3 egg yolks
50 g (2 oz) caster sugar
250 ml (9 fl oz) milk
250 ml (9 fl oz) double cream

75 g (3 oz) granulated sugar
2 tablespoons water
75 ml (3 fl oz) double cream

METHOD

Preheat the oven to 200°C (400°F, Gas 6, 170 Circotherm). Place the almonds on a baking tray and cook in the oven for 7–8 minutes until golden, keep them whole. Roast the hazelnuts in the same way and chop roughly.

Combine the granulated sugar and water in a heavy based pan. Cook slowly to dissolve the sugar. Brush down the sides of the pan with a clean pastry brush dipped in water. Increase the heat and cook without stirring to a golden caramel. Add the roasted almonds and stir once to ensure they are evenly coated. Pour onto a lightly oiled baking tray and leave to cool.

Whisk the egg yolks and caster sugar until thick and pale. In a small pan bring the milk to the boil, pour a little onto the eggs, stir to blend then return to the remainder of the milk in the pan. Cook, stirring until the custard thickens just enough to coat the back of the spoon. Do not allow to boil or it will curdle. Transfer to a bowl to cool.

In the small bowl of a food processor, or with a pestle and mortar, work the almonds and caramel until coarsely ground. Whisk the cream to soft peaks.

Add half the praline to the custard and churn in an ice cream machine until semi-frozen. Add the remaining praline and whipped cream, churn until well mixed and frozen. Transfer to a freezerproof container and freeze until required. Place the remaining granulated sugar and water in a small pan and cook to a pale golden caramel as before. Add the cream and roughly chopped hazelnuts. Stir until smooth. Keep warm or reheat.

Serve balls of the ice cream with the warm sauce poured over them.

Serves 6

THE ULTIMATE CHOCOLATE GATEAU

This flourless cake is truly moist and delicious. Ideally it should be made a day or two before serving and kept refrigerated to allow the flavours to mature. Use a good quality chocolate; the higher the proportion of cocoa solids the better your cake will taste.

INGREDIENTS

200 g (7 oz) plain chocolate, broken into squares
2 tablespoons milk
1 tablespoon brandy
120 g (4¼ oz) butter
4 eggs, separated
120 g (4¼ oz) caster sugar
120 g (4¼ oz) ground almonds

60 g (2½ oz) plain chocolate, broken into squares
25 ml (1 fl oz) milk
1 egg, separated
15 g (½ oz) caster sugar

2 tablespoons apricot jam

200 ml (7 fl oz) whipping cream
1 tablespoon brandy
200 g (7 oz) plain chocolate, broken into squares

grated chocolate or chocolate curls to decorate, if desired

METHOD

Preheat the oven to 180°C (350°F, Gas 4, 160 Circotherm). Grease two 20 cm (8 in) sandwich tins and line the bases with discs of greaseproof paper. Dust with flour. Place the chocolate squares, milk, brandy and butter in a bowl and stand over a pan of gently simmering water. Do not allow the base to come into contact with the water below. Heat slowly until the chocolate has melted. Stir to blend. Remove from the heat and stir in the egg yolks one by one along with half the sugar. Whisk the egg whites to stiff peaks, then fold in the remaining sugar. Fold the ground almonds into the chocolate mixture along with a spoonful of the egg whites. Fold in the remaining egg whites until just mixed.

Divide the mixture between the two sandwich tins. Level the tops and bake in the preheated oven for 15–20 minutes. Leave to cool for 10 minutes before turning onto a wire rack to cool completely.

Meanwhile, make the mousse. Place the chocolate squares and milk in a small bowl and melt over hot water as before. Remove from the heat and stir to blend. Stir in the egg yolk and cool slightly. Whisk the egg white to stiff peaks, then fold in the sugar. Lightly and carefully fold into the chocolate mixture. Use this mousse to sandwich the two layers of cake together. Warm the jam and brush evenly over the top and sides of the cake. Chill the whole thing in the refrigerator for 1 hour or more.

To make the ganache, pour the cream and brandy into a small pan and bring to the boil. Remove the cream from the heat and add the chocolate squares. Leave to stand for 5 minutes without stirring. By now the chocolate should be soft. Stir gently to blend. If you have any small lumps of unmelted chocolate heat gently over a pan of simmering wate. Cool the ganache slightly.

Stand the cake on a wire rack over a clean tray. Slowly pour the ganache over to cover the cake top and sides completely. Have a palette knife at hand just in case you miss any bits. It is possible to patch up any gaps with a little of the ganache that has fallen onto the tray below. Chill until required. Serve either plain or decorated with grated chocolate or chocolate curls, following the recipe on page 171.

Serves 10

WHITE AND DARK CHOCOLATE ROULADE

This moist and decadent dessert improves on keeping so I often make it a day or two before I intend to serve it. Keep it well wrapped and in the fridge. I have to admit, it is hard to resist the temptation to have a small slice every time the door is opened.

INGREDIENTS

175 g (6 oz) plain chocolate
5 eggs, separated
175 g (6 oz) caster sugar
2 tablespoons brandy

110 g (4 oz) white chocolate
200 ml (7 fl oz) double cream
icing sugar for dusting

dark and white chocolate curls
  (optional)

METHOD

Preheat the oven to 180°C (350°F, Gas 4, 160 Circotherm). Line a 33 x 23 cm (13 x 9 in) swiss roll tin with greaseproof paper and brush with melted butter.

Break the plain chocolate into small pieces and place in a small bowl. Stand over a pan of gently simmering water. Ensure the bowl does not touch the water below and does not get too hot. As soon as the chocolate is soft remove the bowl and stir once or twice.

Meanwhile beat the egg yolks and caster sugar until thick and pale. Add the brandy then fold in the melted chocolate. Whisk the egg whites to soft peaks. Stir a spoonful into the chocolate mixture to loosen it, then fold in the remainder. Pour into the prepared tin and bake for 15–20 minutes until springy to the touch but not at all crisp. Remove from the oven and cover with a clean tea towel. Leave to cool. It can be left overnight at this stage.

Chop half the white chocolate into very small pieces and melt the remainder in a small bowl as before. Whip the cream to the ribbon stage and fold in the two chocolates. Lay a large sheet of greaseproof paper on the work surface and dust liberally with icing sugar. Turn the roulade onto the greaseproof paper with the long sides facing you. Peel away the base paper and trim any crisp edges.

Spread the white chocolate cream evenly over the roulade to within 2.5 cm (1 in) of the long side furthest from you. Fold 1 cm (½ in) of the side nearest you over then, with the aid of the paper, and roll the roulade as tightly and evenly as you can. For every roll forward, bring it half a roll back. This helps to tighten it. Wrap the roll in the greaseproof paper and twist the ends like a sweet wrapper to keep it firm. Chill for several hours or overnight.

Decorate the top of the roulade with chocolate curls. Use a potato peeler to shave curls of dark and white chocolate and dust with a little extra icing sugar. Alternatively, make chocolate curls following the recipe on page 00. Slice the roulade with a fine serrated knife wiping the blade clean between each cut.

Serves 8

CHOCOLATE BROWNIE TRUFFLE CAKE

It's really worth investing in a good quality chocolate for this cake. I use Menier or Valrhona, both have a high proportion of cocoa solids and a delicious flavour. Melt it over a bain-marie; always check that the base of your bowl is not touching the water below. This chocolate brownie mixture can be baked in a square tin and cut into squares to serve for tea. Try adding 25 g (1 oz) of chopped walnuts or pecans for extra flavour.

INGREDIENTS

180 g (6 oz) plain chocolate
150 g (5 oz) butter
125 g (4½ oz) caster sugar
2 whole eggs, beaten
50 g (2 oz) plain flour
½ teaspoon baking powder
**25 g (1 oz) plain chocolate,
  chopped in chunks**

425 g (15 oz) plain chocolate
**425 ml (15 fl oz) whipping
  cream**
2 tablespoons brandy

plain chocolate curls (page 171)
1–2 teaspoons cocoa

**sour cream or vanilla ice
  cream if desired**

METHOD

Butter a 22 cm (8½ in) springform tin and line the base with a circle of grease-proof paper. Preheat the oven to 180°C (350°F, Gas 4, 160 Circotherm).

Break the chocolate into squares and place in the bowl with the butter and sugar. Stand over a pan of boiling water. Turn off the heat and leave for 5–10 minutes or until the chocolate and butter have melted and the sugar has dissolved. Stir to blend, remove the bowl from the pan and add the beaten eggs. Mix well to form a smooth batter.

Sieve together the flour and baking powder. Fold into the chocolate mixture with the chopped chocolate chunks. Spoon into the prepared tin. Level the surface with a spoon and bake in the preheated oven for 30–35 minutes. Leave in the tin for 5 minutes, then remove and place on a wire rack to cool.

With a serrated knife carefully slice the brownie in half horizontally. If it starts to crack refrigerate it for an hour or so. This should firm it up. Place the bottom half, cut side up, back into the cleaned springform tin.

Break the remaining chocolate into squares and melt in a bowl over a pan of hot water. Whisk the cream until it just begins to leave a ribbon, add the melted chocolate and the brandy, whisk to mix. Do not overwhisk; it will suddenly thicken. Pour into the tin and top with the remaining brownie half. Chill in the refrigerator for at least 1 hour. If you do overwhisk, simply place the bowl over the pan of warm water, leave for a few moments and stir gently until softened.

Dip a small knife in boiling water and run around the inside of the cake tin, open the clip and remove the brownie. Decorate the top with chocolate curls and dust lightly with cocoa powder. Serve with sour cream or vanilla ice cream.

This dessert actually improves with keeping. It will last for up to 4 days in the refrigerator.

Serves 12

CHOCOLATE PROFITEROLES

I It is essential to dry out the buns thoroughly to prevent them from being soft and limp. Making a small hole in the base serves a double purpose. Firstly it allows the steam to escape, aiding the drying out process, and secondly it provides the perfect place for the filling. The quantities for the chocolate sauce are just right for a warm sauce. If you prefer to serve it cold add a further 50 ml (2 fl oz) of cream. Choux pastry is simple to prepare and versatile.

INGREDIENTS

125 ml (4½ fl oz) water
50 g (2 oz) butter, diced
pinch of salt
1 teaspoon caster sugar
75 g (3 oz) plain flour
2 eggs

300 ml (11 fl oz) whipping
   cream

100 g (3¾ oz) plain chocolate
100 ml (3¾ fl oz) whipping
   cream
1 knob butter

METHOD

Preheat the oven to 200°C (400°F, Gas 6, 170 Circotherm). Butter a large baking tray. Pour the water into a small pan. Add the diced butter, along with the salt and sugar. Place the pan over a moderate heat and cook without boiling until the butter has melted. Sieve the flour onto a piece of paper. Bring the water and butter to a rolling boil and shoot in all the flour whilst beating with a wooden spoon. Turn off the heat and continue beating the mixture until it forms a smooth ball and leaves the sides of the pan. Leave to cool for 5 minutes. Beat the eggs then gradually mix into the dough, beating between each addition. When they are fully incorporated continue beating for 2–3 minutes.

Spoon into a piping bag fitted with a plain 1 cm (½ in) nozzle and pipe choux buns, the size of a walnut, onto the buttered baking tray. Space them well apart as they will expand during cooking.

Dip your finger into cold water and lightly press down any little peaks left at the top. Bake for 25–30 minutes until golden brown and crisp.

Remove the tray from the oven and use a skewer to make a small hole in the base of each bun. Lay them on their sides and return to the oven for 5 minutes to dry out inside. Transfer to a wire rack to cool.

Whip the cream to soft peaks and using a piping bag fitted with a small nozzle pipe in enough to fill each profiterole. Arrange piled up on a dish. Grate the chocolate into a small bowl and add the cream. Stand over a pan of simmering water ensuring the bowl does not touch the water below. When the chocolate is soft stir just enough to blend, add the butter and stir again. Pour the warm sauce over the profiteroles just before serving.

Serves 6–8

CHOCOLATE AND CHERRY CHEESECAKE

My preference has always been for baked cheesecakes over the gelatine-set versions. If fresh cherries are not available use dried cherries, cranberries or blueberries. Soak them in water and kirsch until they become soft and plump, then drain and dry them before adding to the cheesecake.

INGREDIENTS

150 g (5 oz) plain chocolate
   digestive biscuits
25 g (1 oz) plain chocolate
25 g (1 oz) butter

250 g (9 oz) curd cheese
250 g (9 oz) cream cheese
zest and juice of 1 lemon
3 eggs
125 g (4½ oz) caster sugar
1 teaspoon vanilla extract
350 g (12 oz) cherries
1 dessertspoon plain flour
100 g (3¾ oz) plain chocolate

450 g (1 lb) cherries
1 tablespoon water
50 g (2 oz) caster sugar
2 teaspoons cornflour
2 tablespoons kirsch

METHOD

Lightly butter a 22 cm (8½ in) springform tin and dust it with flour. Crush the digestive biscuits either in a food processor or by putting them in a bowl and crushing them with the end of a rolling pin or pestle.

Break the chocolate into squares and place in a small bowl with the butter. Stand this over a pan of gently simmering water. Do not allow the base of the bowl to come into contact with the water or the chocolate will overheat. After 3–4 minutes stir the melted mixture to blend.

Pour the chocolate onto the crushed biscuits and mix until all the pieces are evenly coated. Spread the biscuits evenly over the base of the tin. Press down with the back of a spoon. Chill in the refrigerator whilst preparing the batter.

Preheat the oven to 180°C (350°F, Gas 4, 160 Circotherm). Sieve the cheeses together into a large bowl. Add the lemon zest and juice. Beat the eggs and stir into the cheeses with the sugar and vanilla extract. Beat well to form a smooth batter. Wash the cherries and dry well; remove the stones. Toss with flour. Chop the chocolate into small pieces and fold into the batter with the cherries.

Pour the cheesecake mixture into the biscuit-lined tin and bake for 35–40 minutes. Turn off the oven and, leaving the door ajar, allow the cheesecake to cool inside. Chill overnight in the refrigerator.

The following day wash, halve and stone the remaining cherries and place in a pan with the water and sugar. Cover and set on a gentle heat for 7–10 minutes to cook the cherries lightly and let their juices run. In a small bowl or ramekin mix together the cornflour and kirsch, add a little of the hot cherry liquid, stir back into the cherries, bring to the boil and cook for 30 seconds. Turn the cherries onto a large dish to cool.

To serve, carefully loosen the sides of the cheesecake and unclip the tin. With the aid of a palette knife slide the cheesecake onto your serving plate. Top with the cooked cherries and serve cut into wedges.

Serves 8–10

CHESTNUT TORTE

Although I always think it would be wonderful to make this from whole fresh chestnuts just to get in the seasonal spirit, somehow time never allows. Fortunately cans of chestnut purée are now easy to find in supermarkets. For this recipe use the unsweetened variety. Marrons glacés are whole chestnuts that have been cooked and soaked in a sugar syrup until they are moist and candied. They are an expensive luxury and, if you prefer, simply decorate the torte with the cream and omit the marrons.

INGREDIENTS

25 g (1 oz) butter
100 g (3¾ oz) plain chocolate,
  broken into squares
1 tablespoon brandy
1 tablespoon golden syrup
125 g (4½ oz) shortbread

1 sachet (11 g/0.4 oz) gelatine
2 tablespoons water
450 g (1 lb) granulated sugar
150 ml (5 fl oz) water
275 g (10 oz) unsweetened
  chestnut purée
200 ml (7 fl oz) whipping
  cream
250 g (9 oz) marscapone

25 ml (1 fl oz) whipping cream
25 g (1 oz) plain chocolate,
  broken into squares

200 ml (7 fl oz) whipping
  cream
8 marrons glacés

METHOD

Place the butter, chocolate squares, brandy and golden syrup in a bowl over a pan of simmering water. Heat gently, not allowing the bowl to touch the water below, until the chocolate is melted. Remove from the heat and stir to blend.

Roughly crush the shortbread and stir into the chocolate mixture. Spoon into a 22 cm (8½ in) springform tin. Spread evenly to cover the base. Chill.

Mix the gelatine with the water in a small bowl. Leave to soak.

Combine the sugar and water in a heavy based pan. Cook gently to dissolve the sugar, bring to the boil and cook for a further 3 minutes. Turn off the heat and cool for 2 minutes. Add the soaked gelatine and stir to dissolve.

Place the chestnut purée in a bowl and slowly beat in the sugar syrup until smooth. This is easiest with an electric whisk. If you have persistent lumps pass the mixture through a sieve. Leave on one side to cool. Stir from time to time to ensure it does not set in lumps. Whip the cream to very soft peaks and fold into the marscapone, then fold in the chestnut purée and pour over the biscuit mixture in the springform tin.

Put the cream and chocolate squares in a small bowl. Stand over a pan of simmering water and leave until the chocolate is soft. Stir to blend. Spoon teaspoonfuls of the chocolate cream onto the top of the torte. It should not be set at this stage. Then use a skewer or small knife to swirl and marble it into the top of the chestnut mixture. Chill for several hours or overnight.

Remove the torte from the tin and transfer to a serving plate. Decorate the top with whipped cream and the marrons glacés.

Serves 8

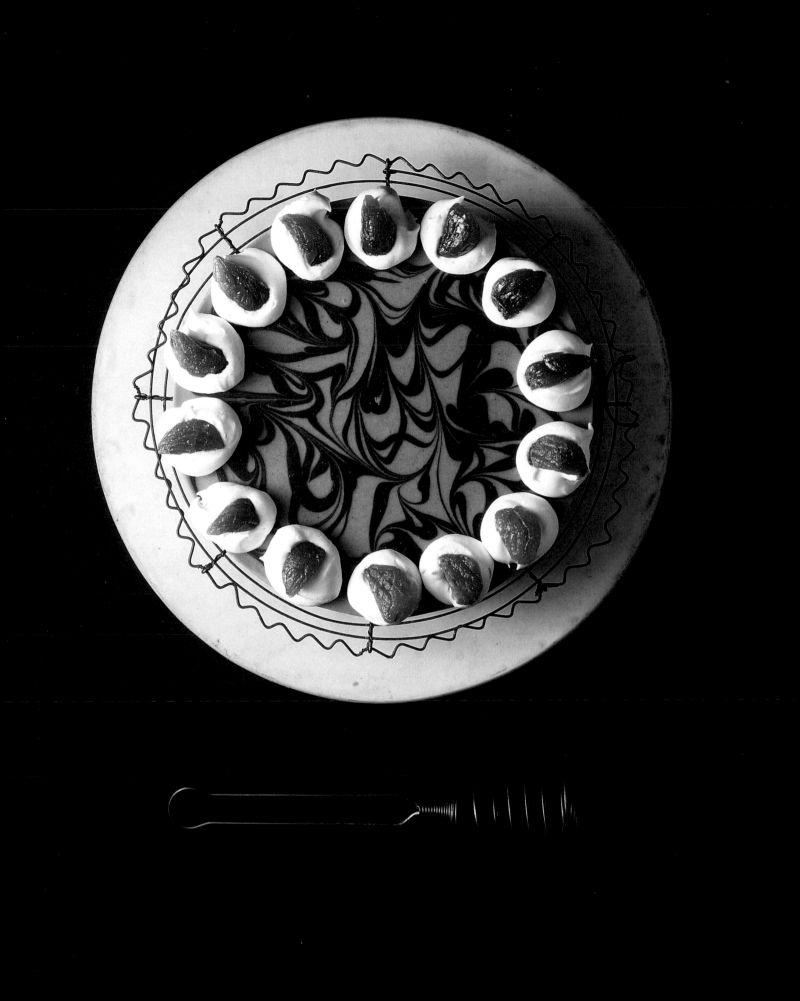

BRANDIED CHERRIES DIPPED IN CHOCOLATE

Although not strictly a dessert, these cherries are a real indulgence at the end of a special meal. If the menu has been very rich, perhaps you would prefer to serve the cherries instead of a pudding. They are a delicious accompaniment to coffee. Although cherries are not in season at this time of year, there are often some good, if a little pricey, imports available around Christmas time. Use the best quality chocolate you can find.

INGREDIENTS

225 g (8 oz) cherries on stems
200 ml (7 fl oz) brandy
100 g (3¾ oz) dark chocolate

METHOD

Wash the cherries, leaving the stems attached. Dry them well then, using a stainless steel pin, prick each one 6–8 times right through to the stone.

Place the cherries in a bowl and pour over the brandy. Cover with a plate. Leave for 24 hours turning them occasionally so they absorb the alcohol. Drain the cherries and dry on kitchen paper. Reserve the alcohol.

Break the chocolate into small pieces and place in a bowl with 1–2 tablespoons of the reserved brandy. Stand over a pan of gently simmering water to melt. Ensure the water does not touch the base of the bowl and that it does not get too hot as this will burn the chocolate. Stir to blend and remove from the heat.

Holding the cherries by the stems, dip each one into the chocolate. Let any excess chocolate fall back into the bowl. Stand the cherries on a tray lined with greaseproof paper and leave to cool and harden.

Serves 6–8

CAPPUCCINO MOUSSE

This light and airy mousse resembles a cappuccino when served in coffee cups. If you do not have enough cups to go round, buy ready-made chocolate cups and serve it in those. I do not recommend omitting the coffee liqueur in this recipe as it really adds to the flavour. If you do not want to splash out and buy a full bottle, look out for the miniatures available in many off-licences. Tia Maria is made in Jamaica from coffee grown in the Blue Mountains.

INGREDIENTS

½ **sachet gelatine (5 g/0.2 oz)**
1 **tablespoon water**
2 **eggs, separated**
75 g (3 oz) **caster sugar**
2 **tablespoons Tia Maria**
   or Kalhua
1 **dessertspoon instant coffee**
   mixed with 1 tablespoon
   boiling water
250 ml (9 fl oz) **double cream**

cocoa or chocolate shavings

METHOD

Soak the gelatine in the water in a small pan. Place the egg yolks and sugar in a large bowl. Add the Tia Maria and the coffee. Stand the bowl over a pan of gently simmering water. Do not allow the base of the bowl to come into direct contact with the water. Whisk continually until thick and the mixture forms a ribbon when a little is allowed to fall back on itself. Remove the bowl from the heat and continue whisking until cold.

Melt the gelatine over a low heat and stir into the egg mixture, being careful not to knock out any of the air.

Whip the cream to soft peaks and fold 150 ml (5 fl oz) into the mousse.

Clean and dry the whisk, then whip the egg whites to soft peaks. Fold lightly into the mousse.

Spoon the mixture into six coffee cups and refrigerate until set. Spoon the reserved cream on top of the mousses and dust with a little cocoa or a few shavings of chocolate.

Serves 6

BAKED TAMARILLOS WITH VANILLA SEED ICE CREAM AND CHOCOLATE CHIP COOKIES

E*xtremely high in Vitamin C these egg-shaped, orangy-red tree tomatoes can be very acidic when raw. Eaten warm their succulent, sweetened flesh is delicious with the melting vanilla ice cream. The seeds are edible although I prefer to remove them, along with the skin, and indulge in the flesh only.*

INGREDIENTS

500 ml (18 fl oz) milk
2 vanilla pods, split
6 egg yolks
125 g (4½ oz) caster sugar
250 ml (9 fl oz) double cream

125 g (4½ oz) plain flour
¼ teaspoon bicarbonate
   of soda
pinch of salt
80 g (3 oz) butter
80 g (3 oz) soft brown sugar
1 egg
1 teaspoon vanilla extract
50 g (2 oz) whole unpeeled
   hazelnuts
110 g (4 oz) plain chocolate

6 tamarillos
icing sugar

METHOD

First make the vanilla ice cream. Pour the milk into a small pan with the split vanilla pods. Place over heat and bring to the boil. In a bowl whisk together the egg yolks and caster sugar until thick and pale. Pour a little of the boiling milk onto the yolks, stir to blend, then return to the milk pan. Cook slowly whilst continually stirring until the custard thickens to coat the back of the spoon. Do not allow it to boil or it will curdle. Transfer to a bowl to cool. Remove the vanilla pods, squeezing or scraping out the little black seeds into the custard as you go. Whip the cream to soft peaks. Transfer the custard to an ice cream machine and churn until semi-frozen. Add the cream and continue churning until frozen. Transfer to a freezerproof container and freeze until required.

To make the cookies, preheat the oven to 190°C (375°F, Gas 5, 160 Circotherm). Grease two large baking trays. Sieve the flour with the bicarbonate of soda and salt. Soften the butter and place in a bowl with the soft brown sugar. Beat until soft and light. Whisk the egg, then gradually beat into the batter with the vanilla extract. Fold in the flour. Coarsely chop the unpeeled hazelnuts. Cut the chocolate into rough chunks. Fold both into the dough.

Place heaped dessertspoonfuls of the mixture, spaced well apart, onto the prepared trays. Flatten slightly with a spoon. You should make twelve cookies. Bake in the preheated oven for 10–12 minutes until golden. Transfer to a wire rack to cool, then store in an airtight container. Keep the oven hot.

Remove the stalks from the tamarillos, then with a sharp knife score a cross through the skin at the top and bottom of each fruit. Bring a large pan of water to the boil and have ready a basin of cold water and a slotted spoon. Dip the fruits into the boiling water for 30 seconds. Then, using the spoon, transfer them quickly to the cold water. Leave for a few seconds before peeling away the skin. Remove the seeds if you wish.

Cut each tamarillo in half lengthwise and lay the halves, cut sides up, in a single layer in an ovenproof dish. Dredge generously with icing sugar. Bake at 190°C (375°F, Gas 5, 160 Circotherm) for 15–20 minutes until the fruit is soft and the juices are beginning to run. Serve warm with vanilla ice cream and the cookies.

Serves 6

CHARLOTTE MALAKOFF

T his charlotte is extremely rich, so a little goes a very long way. It is delicious served with fruits. At this time of year there are plenty of bottled fruits available to buy – try cherries, raspberries or clementines. A charlotte was originally a French dessert. Those made in a charlotte russe (or mould) such as this one, are believed to be the invention of the great chef and writer, Antonin Carême, who was working in the early part of the nineteenth century. Sponge or lady fingers were used to line the mould, which was then filled with bavarois or crème chantilly. This makes an interesting change from the traditional dish.

INGREDIENTS

12 sponge fingers
1 tablespoon kirsch
1 tablespoon water
125 g (4½ oz) butter, softened
125 g (4½ oz) icing sugar
125 g (4½ oz) ground almonds
125 ml (4½ fl oz) whipping cream
25 ml (1 fl oz) kirsch

450 g (1 lb) frozen raspberries
icing sugar
juice of ½ lemon

icing sugar for dusting

METHOD

Brush the flat sides of the sponge fingers with a little of the kirsch mixed with the water and use to line (sugared side out) the base and sides of a 570 ml (1 pint) charlotte mould or soufflé dish.

Soften the butter and cream it with the icing sugar until pale and light. Fold in the ground almonds, the lightly whipped cream and the kirsch. Spoon into the lined mould pressing down well to ensure you have no gaps or air pockets. Trim any biscuits that stand above the filling; cover with clingfilm and chill for at least two hours.

To make the raspberry sauce, pass the fruit through a sieve to remove the pips and sweeten to taste with icing sugar. Add a few drops of lemon juice to enhance the flavour.

Turn out the charlotte and dust with a little icing sugar. Serve in thin slices with the raspberry sauce and your chosen fruit.

Serves 8

BAKED RICE PUDDING

A good old-fashioned pudding. Here it is enriched with cream although if you prefer a lighter version double the quantity of milk and omit the cream. Left undisturbed in the oven the rice swells and absorbs much of the liquid and a wonderful golden skin forms on the top. Rice puddings are made with short-grained rice.

INGREDIENTS

25 g (1 oz) butter
50 g (2 oz) pudding rice
  (Carolina)
570 ml (1 pint) milk
570 ml (1 pint) single cream
2 vanilla pods, split
2–4 tablespoons caster sugar

fruit purée or jam

METHOD

Preheat the oven to 150°C (300°F, Gas 2, 140 Circotherm). Generously butter a 1.2 litre (2 pint) baking dish. Choose one that is also suitable as a serving dish.

Sprinkle the rice over the base of the dish. Heat the milk and cream with the split vanilla pods and sugar until it reaches boiling point. Strain over the rice, give it a good stir, then bake undisturbed for 2–2½ hours.

The rice should be soft and creamy and the top golden brown.

A little extra cream or milk can be poured through a slit in the skin and allowed to warm through when the cooking is completed if the pudding seems too dry. Serve with a spoonful of fruit purée or jam.

Serves 6

LAST-MINUTE CHRISTMAS PUDDING

As a rule, a Christmas pudding should be made six months to a year before it is eaten. The longer it is kept in a cool, dark place the more it matures. Although not strictly last-minute, you will see that as with all Christmas puddings this one requires rather lengthy cooking and the fruits need prior soaking. It can be made a day or so before serving and will still be deliciously rich and moist. Once the pudding has had its initial cooking it can be kept in its basin, re-covered and stored until required. To reheat simply steam as before for 2 hours.

INGREDIENTS

150 g (5 oz) raisins
150 g (5 oz) sultanas
50 g (2 oz) dried cranberries
  or raisins
50 g (2 oz) currants
50 g (2 oz) dried sour cherries
50 g (2 oz) mixed peel
200 ml (7 fl oz) brown ale
  or stout
2 tablespoons brandy or whisky
1 large cooking apple

50 g (2 oz) self-raising flour
1½ teaspoons mixed spice
110 g (4 oz) vegetable suet
110 g (4 oz) fresh wholemeal
  breadcrumbs
150 g (5 oz) molasses sugar
50 g (2 oz) chopped almonds
zest and juice of 1 lemon
1 tablespoon treacle
2 eggs, beaten

extra brandy for flaming
200 ml (7 fl oz) double cream

METHOD

Combine the dried fruits and mixed peel in a large pan, pour over the brown ale or stout and bring to the boil. Remove the pan from the heat and stir in the brandy. Cover with a cloth and leave in a cool place overnight. Stir once or twice if possible.

Grate the apple, unpeeled, and stir into the fruits.

Sieve the flour and mixed spice into a large bowl. Add the suet and bread-crumbs along with the sugar, chopped almonds and lemon zest. Stir to mix.

Stir together the lemon juice, the treacle and the beaten eggs. Mix into the dry ingredients along with the soaked fruits and any remaining juices.

Pack into a well greased 1.5 litre (2½ pint) pudding basin. Cover with a double layer of buttered greaseproof paper. Then cover with a pudding cloth or a circle of tinfoil which overhangs the top of the basin by 7.5 cm (3 in). Make a 1 cm (½ in) pleat in the foil then place it over the basin and tie securely with string. The pleat allows for expansion during cooking. I find it useful to leave the string long and use the excess to form a handle or loop which makes lifting the pudding easier.

Stand the basin on a trivet inside a large pan. Pour in enough water to come 5 cm (2 in) up the sides, cover with a tightly fitting lid and steam for 6 hours. It will be necessary to top up the water from time to time.

Snip the string and remove the greaseproof paper and tinfoil. Turn the cooked pudding onto a warm serving plate. Warm a little extra brandy in a ladle, light with a match or taper and pour over the pudding. Serve at once with pouring cream.

Serves 8–10

APPLE AND MINCEMEAT FILO WREATH

This festive wreath is perfect for a Christmas party. Ideally it should be served on the day it is made as filo pastry has a tendency to become soggy if kept for any length of time. I do not recommend Bramley cooking apples for this dish as they cook down quickly and produce a lot of water. Choose either a firm cooking apple such as Howgate Wonder or one of the many varieties of eating apple that are available. You may wish to adjust the quantity of sugar to accommodate the apples you have chosen.

INGREDIENTS

3 large apples
200 g (7 oz) mincemeat
**75 g (3 oz) dried cranberries
   or raisins**
100 g (4 oz) soft brown sugar
2 tablespoons brandy

100 g (4 oz) butter, melted
**10 sheets filo pastry 30 x 45 cm
   (12 x 18 in)**
100 g (4 oz) ground almonds

icing sugar for dusting

extra cranberries
holly leaves
single cream

METHOD

Preheat the oven to 180°C (350°F, Gas 4, 160 Circotherm). Butter a large baking tray. Peel, core and slice the apples. Mix with the mincemeat, cranberries, soft brown sugar and the brandy. Stir well.

Melt the butter. Lay one sheet of filo pastry flat on the work surface. Brush with melted butter and sprinkle with one-sixth of the almonds. Repeat twice more, then lay a fourth sheet of pastry on top.

Spoon half of the apple mixture over the pastry leaving a 5 cm (2 in) border around the edge. Roll the pastry from one of the long sides to enclose all the filling. Shape into a semicircle and place on the baking tray.

Repeat with four more sheets of filo, butter, the remaining almonds and apple mixture. Place the second semicircle onto the same baking tray and tuck the ends together to form a complete circle. Brush the whole thing with melted butter. Cut one of the last two sheets of filo in half and use to wrap around the joins on the filo ring. Brush with a little butter.

Cut the remaining sheet of filo into stars using a small pastry cutter. Brush with butter and place decoratively on top of the ring. Bake for 35–40 minutes until golden.

Dust with icing sugar and decorate with a few cranberries and holly leaves before serving warm with plenty of fresh cream.

Serves 8–10

BASIC RECIPES

PATE FEUILLETEE (PUFF PASTRY)

200 g (7 oz) plain flour
½ teaspoon salt
25 g (1 oz) butter
100 ml (3¾ fl oz) cold water
175 g (6 oz) butter, softened

Sieve the flour and salt into a bowl. Rub the butter into the flour. Make a well in the centre, then pour in the water. Mix in the flour and work gently to a dough. Wrap in greaseproof paper and chill in the fridge for 20 minutes.

Place the ball of dough onto a lightly floured work surface. Roll into a four-point star approximately 30 cm (12 in) across. The centre of the star should be thicker than the points. Place the softened butter onto the thicker centre part and wrap over the four points to make a parcel. The thicker base of the dough compensates for the four layers on top of the butter, making it even.

Bat the dough very lightly with the rolling pin to spread the butter then roll into a rectangle approximately 14 cm (5½ in) by 41 cm (16 in). Fold in three, then turn the dough round at a right angle so that the opening is on your right. Repeat the rolling, folding and turning once more so the dough has had two turns. Rest in the fridge for 20 minutes.

Repeat the rolling, folding and turning twice more until the dough has had four turns in all. The dough is now ready to use and can be wrapped and refrigerated for 24 hours or frozen for up to 1 month.

When ready to use the dough, repeat the rolling, folding and turning twice more giving the pastry six turns in all. These last two should always be carried out just before use.

PATE SUCREE (SWEET SHORTCAKE PASTRY)

200 g (7 oz) plain flour
pinch of salt
50 g (2 oz) caster sugar
100 g (3¾ oz) butter
2 egg yolks
1 teaspoon vanilla extract
1 tablespoon water

Sieve the flour and salt onto a large clean area of your work surface. A piece of marble is perfect, but not essential, for making pastry as it keeps everything cool. With a ramekin or small bowl work the flour from the centre in a circular motion, to create a large well. Keep going until you have a ring of flour approximately 46 cm (18 in) in diameter. Sprinkle the sugar just inside the flour to give an inner, slightly smaller ring.

Soften the butter and break it into small pieces, place in the centre of the ring along with the egg yolks, vanilla extract and water.

Using your fingers or, if you have one, a plastic baker's card, work the eggs and butter until they resemble fine scrambled eggs.

Bring in the sugar and work briefly. Using the baker's card or a palette knife bring in all the flour, chopping and turning through the butter as you go. Continue chopping and turning until everything is well mixed and close to coming together. Now is the time to add a little more water if you think the dough is going to be too dry. I usually find it is not required.

This is the fun part: using the heel of your hand lightly push the dough down and away from you. Do this thoroughly but once only, overworking will only make the pastry tough. Now bring the dough together and work lightly into a ball. Wrap in greaseproof paper or clingfilm and refrigerate for 30 minutes before using, or wrap well and freeze until required.

TO MAKE ICE CREAM OR SORBET WITHOUT AN ICE CREAM MACHINE

Make the custard or ice cream base in exactly the same way as usual. Instead of pouring into an ice cream machine pour the mixture into a shallow plastic tub, approximately 2 litre (3½ pint) capacity.

Cover with a lid or a piece of foil and place in the coldest part of your freezer for 2–3 hours. By this time the outside of the mixture should be frozen and the centre still liquid. Remove the tub from the freezer and, using a hand-held electric whisk or a balloon whisk if you do not have the former, beat the mixture until it becomes a smooth slush. Add the lightly whipped cream or whisked egg whites at this point. Return the tub to the freezer and leave for a further 2 hours. Repeat the beating and freezing process until the mixture is fully frozen.

It is hard to be precise on timings as all freezers vary. Until you have made ice cream a few times you may find it best to check it fairly regularly.

Remember to transfer your ice cream or sorbet to the fridge for approximately 30 minutes before serving. This softens it slightly and makes scooping easier.

TO BAKE BLIND

Preheat the oven to 180°C (350°F, Gas 4, 160 Circotherm). Roll the well chilled dough into a circle slightly larger than the tin you are using. This allows for the pastry to come up the sides with a little over. With the aid of the rolling pin lay the pastry over the greased tin. Use your fingers to press the dough well into the base and sides. Work from the centre outwards so you do not trap any air. Remove any excess pastry by rolling over the top of the tin with the rolling pin. Prick the base well with a fork. Chill for 15–30 minutes. Line the pastry case with a disc of greaseproof paper and fill with baking beans. Place on a baking tray (this makes carrying easier) and bake for 10 minutes. Remove the baking beans and paper and bake for a further 10 minutes. If your filling is very liquid, eg. the blood orange tart on page 29, it is advisable to brush the inside of the cooked tart case with a little beaten egg. Bake for 1 minute, then repeat. This gives the pastry a waterproof lining and prevents it from going soggy. The tart case can be kept in an airtight container for a day at this stage if required.

TO MAKE CHOCOLATE CURLS

There are many ways of making chocolate curls. The easiest method to make small curls and shavings is simply to take a large block of chocolate that has been left at room temperature. With a potato peeler, shave the sides of the block and curls will form. If the curls crack, warm the chocolate a little in your hands and try again.

The second method requires chocolate coating rather than good quality chocolate. This is the cheaper chocolate substitute sold in most supermarkets. It is made from a base of vegetable oil making it more flexible than real chocolate. Its flavour is not wonderful, but used in small amounts as a decoration it is perfectly adequate.

Break the chocolate coating (plain, milk or white) into squares and place in a bowl over a pan of gently simmering water. Ensure the base of the bowl does not come into contact with the water below or the chocolate coating may overheat. As soon as the chocolate has melted, remove it from the pan of water, wipe the base of the bowl dry as you do this is to avoid any drips falling into the chocolate and spoiling its texture. Pour the chocolate onto a clean, dry marble slab or work surface. Use a large metal palate knife and spread the chocolate as smoothly as possible until it is approximately 2 mm (⅛ in) thick. Leave until just set, then use a large knife held at a 30 degree angle and push the chocolate away from you. Large curls and scrolls will form. Store the curls in an airtight container until ready to use.

The final type of curls require chocolate couverture. This is good quality chocolate made with cocoa butter. To make the chocolate pliable and glossy it needs to be tempered. Grate the chocolate into a bowl and melt it over a bain-marie as above. Heat the chocolate until it reaches 45°C (115°F). Stir the chocolate to ensure it is smooth then pour onto a clean, dry marble slab or work surface. Ensure no drips of water get into the chocolate. Using a large palate knife work the chocolate backwards and forwards until it reaches the point of setting. Quickly scrape the chocolate back into the bowl and heat again, stirring continually until it reaches 32°C (90°F) for plain chocolate and 29°C (85°F) for milk or white chocolate. Pour onto the marble slab and use to make curls, as per previous method.

INDEX

ACKNOWLEDGMENTS

During the writing of this book, there have been many people whose enthusiasm and encouragement have been a great support. Most notably my husband Tim who was happy to put aside his fitness regime in order to sample over one hundred desserts. His favourable and sometimes not so favourable comments were greatly received. My daughter Holly who although not born until this book was almost finished has also, unbeknown to her, sampled most of the recipes with me. I hope she does not grow up with too sweet a tooth.

My thanks goes to my parents for passing their love of good food to me, and particularly to my mother for testing many of the recipes. I would like to thank Miranda Williams for typing the manuscript and Bud MacLennan for editing it. My agent Jacqueline Korn for believing in the idea when all around people were looking for low fat alternatives! Many thanks to Jess Koppel for her help in the early stages of this project.

My thanks goes also to Sara Taylor for creating such tempting photographs. To Jacques and Maxine Clarke for making the food look truly delicious and to Wei Tang for searching out many interesting props. Finally I would like to thank Kyle and her team for all their hard work.